HOW WE UNDERST
The Surviv

ALAN MACFARLANE was born in Shillong, India, in 1941 and educated at the Dragon School, Sedbergh School, Oxford and London Universities. He is the author of over twenty published books, including *The Origins of English Individualism* (1978) and *Letters to Lily: On How the World Works* (2005). He has worked in England, Nepal, Japan and China as both an historian and anthropologist.

He was elected to the British Academy in 1986 and is now Emeritus Professor of Anthropology at the University of Cambridge and a Life Fellow of King's College, Cambridge.

How Can
We Survive?

Thoughts for Taras

8/6/18

With warmest wishes for

[signature]

ALAN MACFARLANE

2018

First published in 2017
Second edition published in 2018 by

Cam Rivers Publishing Ltd
5 Canterbury Close
Cambridge CB4 3QQ

www.cambridgerivers.com
press@cambridgerivers.com

Author: Alan Macfarlane
Series Editor: Zilan Wang
Editor: Sarah Harrison
Marketing Manager: James O'Sullivan
Typesetting and cover design: Jaimie Norman

The Kaifeng Foundation generously supports the publishing of this book

For Taras Petrovic-Šteger, with my love

Alan Macfarlane, 2016

Contents

Why I Am Writing to You

T HERE ARE MANY challenges for you as you grow up in today's world. In this small book I have identified eight of these which seem particularly acute. In each essay I try to outline, usually through a preliminary historical overview, what I think the heart of the problem is. In other words, were we are now and what the choices are. I then make some suggestions of ways in which we may escape from the traps and tendencies.

The suggested solutions are often quite radical and may strike some as either impractical or bizarre, or both. Yet I believe, with Albert Einstein, that 'Unless an idea starts off as absurd, there is no hope for it.' If it is an obvious idea, others will have thought of it, and probably tried it and we are still in our current mess. So we need 'absurd', unlikely, unexpected ideas which make a new strong suggestion. What is sometime called 'blue skies thought'.

The need for radical new initiatives also stems from realizing the truth of another of Einstein's remarks, namely that 'Problems cannot be solved at the same level of thinking that created them.' In other words, we need to rise up to another level of analysis if we are going to survive and thrive. It is no help to go on thinking within the current, sterile and often dangerous current paradigm. It is time for intuitive or imaginative leaps into a new future. Only if we really change direction as we contemplate a very different world ahead, will we avoid various disasters, or at least serious difficulties.

So the essays are to stimulate thought, perhaps cause disagreement and a need for modification. They are an attempt to lift myself, and I hope the reader, out of mental ruts.

The essays were written very quickly, partly inspired by a request to give two seminars for a joint meeting of the Resolution Foundation and the China Media Centre (University of Westminster) in London. Both these organisations are concerned with the intersection between academic ideas and practical problems. They asked me to think about the relations of the family and state, derived from my earlier work on *The Origins of English Individualism* (1978).

As I jotted down some possible ideas for those talks, I found myself expanding into new areas. So I decided to keep the spontaneity of these reflections, and to draw them together as another of my current series of short books, principally written as a series of 'Master's Letters to Young Chinese', published in China.

The other books in this series are more academic, about theory and methods of discovery and creativity. This set aims to apply some of the theories to selected practical issues. If we are to survive, we must learn from our past, and from the huge variety of human experience across the world. Here are a few hints for a rushing, changing and dangerous and unprecedented world.

ONE

Population and Resources

THE FUNDAMENTAL RELATIONSHIP between population and resources was described two centuries ago by Thomas Malthus. In his Essay on the Principle of Population (1798 and a second, enlarged, edition in 1803) Malthus explained that women can, with natural fertility (that is without any use of contraception, and marrying reasonably young) produce an average of at least six live births. With even medium to highish mortality, four of these will survive to adulthood. So each couple will produce an average of four children, thus doubling the population each generation.

By the mathematical law of doubling, you will get what is called exponential, or non-linear, growth of the order of 2: 4: 8: 16: 32: 64. Very soon the numbers become huge. Thus it only took about 34 doublings to move from a hypothetical pair of humans, Adam and Eve we might call them, to our current world population of 7.4 billion people. If we continue at current population levels of growth, doubling say every 30 years, in 200 years the world population will be approaching 500 billion. Another thirty years on and there are 1000 billion!

There have been some signs of slowing of growth rates for various regions. Yet even in my own lifetime, as the rate drops in parts of the world and the One Child Policy reduces growth in China, world population has gone up by threefold in seventy years. When I was born the world population was 2.3 billion, now it is 7.4 billion. Currently it is ten times as great as when Malthus made his calculations.

The rates vary. Western European population has almost stopped growing, apart from immigration, but there is still massive growth in Africa, the Muslim belt and India. For example in India a population of about 288 million in 1901, about 400 million at Independence in 1947, is now over three times that size, at over 1.3 billion.

The other part of Malthus' s argument concerns resources. He looked at a basically agricultural world where it was only possible to increase output of food and other goods rather slowly. He estimated that, at the most optimistic, such resources could increase in a linear rate in each generation – one, two, three, four.

The intersection of the two laws meant that the population would rapidly outstrip resource increases. For example, if unimpeded, from an original situation where population and resources were balanced, after two centuries of increase it would mean that an initial population of one million persons would reach thirty-two million after twelve generations, while original resources to feed the one million would have increased to twelve. The gap would grow faster and faster.

As Malthus looked back over the historical record he could see that this gap has led to the collapse of empires and states and much of the misery of mankind. The gap was periodically closed by catastrophes – what he called the 'positive checks', that is those which act to raise the death rates. These were principally war, famine and disease. Unless population was checked, he believed that there was no escape from the inevitable nightmare.

* * *

Since Malthus wrote there have been two major changes which have not disproved his theory, but made the outcome more complex. The first, which he had advocated, is the widespread control of fertility in many parts of the world. Malthus approved of methods that had long been used in England, Norway and Switzerland, namely natural control through delaying marriages until the later twenties for women, combined with non-marriage and non-reproduction by a large part of the female population, perhaps a quarter or more.

What Malthus did not approve of was what he called 'Vice', namely any form of artificial contraception – both prevention of conception (the predecessors of a condom, Pill, IUD etc) and post conception control – abortion and infanticide. Yet it is precisely this growth of ways of inhibiting conception which has now given many the control over how many children they have. As a result of this, over perhaps half of the surface of the world, delays in marrying as women become educated and go into the labour force, fertility rates have come down to about parity, or two children per couple. Yet there is persistent high fertility in the other half of the world, so population is now still growing, given the absolute size of the population, which is breeding faster than it has ever done in history.

* * *

The second change concerns Malthus's theory about the possible rate of increase in production. Here, two things have happened, one positive and one negative. Malthus, as noted, was only able to envisage an agricultural world expanding slowly, constrained by how much of the sun's energy could be converted by plants and animals for human use. Yet, even as he was writing, a new world of industrial production was emerging for the first time on this planet. This was composed of two new features, which would change, temporarily at least, his laws.

One change was the discovery of vast resources of carbon energy in the form of coal and later of oil, which could be harnessed through machines to produce goods. This unlocked a vast treasure which meant that production could also, at least for a while, grow exponentially, matching population.

The machines themselves were partly made possible by a second development of this period, which was the systematic application of an expanding, increasingly accurate, knowledge of the laws of nature in physics, chemistry and biology. The application included the making of more powerful machines, and the rapid improvements in agricultural production through new fertilisers and improved plants and animals. New plants and ideas, as well as cheap goods, were also flooding into Europe from all over the world as navigation improved, and railways were starting to make the cost of shipping goods much cheaper.

So again, for a century or two, the Malthusian law appeared to be suspended. This more than compensated for the fact that some of the new knowledge was used to rapidly reduce death rates, especially in infancy, from epidemic and endemic disease. The rapid drop in mortality, and the gradual elimination of famine, meant that population rocketed in many parts of the world over the next century, even if fertility rates started to drop somewhat.

* * *

Yet if Malthus were writing today he might well argue that while the catastrophes of war, famine and disease, caused by the intersection of population and resources, have been temporarily suspended, we are now much more aware that there are finite limits to economic growth and of the disastrous effects of the endless increase of population.

Malthus would have pointed out that the absolute numbers, growing exponentially, are pressing on all of the Earth's resources in an extreme way because the numbers of people are combined with something he did not anticipate. That is the extraordinary rise in the expectations and standard of living in the quarter of humanity who live with what we might call a Western or modern lifestyle.

The richest quarter of mankind consumes ten times as much per person in the way of resources, with their large houses, meat diets, cars and consumer goods as the rest of the world's population. Even in 2000, it was estimated that the top 16% of the world's population consumed four fifths of the world's resources. The richest ten per cent cause over half of the world's carbon emissions.

Since the aspiration of the other, poorer, four fifths is to join the top fifth, how are we to cope with a world which is still growing by a billion or so every few years, but also where millions are attempting to lift themselves out of poverty?

What, for example, is the effect of the rightly welcomed achievement of the Chinese government in lifting seven hundred million poor farmers in China out of poverty in one generation since 1980? What happens when this tenth of humankind suddenly quadruples its demand for various resources? Or when, as is planned in India, and is already happening in a rich middle-class of perhaps 250 million in the cities, millions and hundreds of millions in India and elsewhere start to consume ten times as much as they did a generation ago? In effect what has happened in just China or India in the last generation has been the equivalent of adding at least two billion people, in terms of consumption, to the planet.

* * *

Although we can now produce so much in 'factories' – whether cars or washing machines, chickens or milk, or increasingly vegetables and proteins, this does not take away the problem of the wider 'externalities' or outside influences of soaring population and higher wealth. Let me just mention a few of the well-known pressure points.

One is the forests. Everyone knows that vast swathes of the last remaining great forests, whether in the Amazon, Central Africa, Indonesia or South East Asia are being destroyed. In the desire to farm crops and animals, the Indonesian and central African and South American jungles and forests are being decimated. In south-east Asia the precious woods are being stripped out for furniture and buildings. In Nepal, China and elsewhere the last forests are being logged for firewood.

Attempts to replace wood in parts of the world - for use as paper, furniture, buildings – with the use of 'sustainable' planting, while admirable, only touch part of the edges of the problem. At present rates, within a generation, most of the forests and jungles will have gone, with huge consequences for biodiversity, animals and plants, as well as the loss of the carbon absorption function of trees.

A similar picture can, of course, be painted for the oceans. The ever greater demand for ocean products, particularly fish, the dumping of chemicals, micro-beads, plastics and sewage, has already depleted many fish stocks and destroyed large swathes of the coral reefs. The story is depressing and though recognising certain success stories of commercial conservation, the pressures of population and higher living standards are unlikely to improve the situation any time soon.

A third well-known cause of concern is the diminishing supplies of fresh water. It is known that a combination of the mounting needs in agriculture and cities is leading to a crisis of water supplies in India and China and elsewhere as the aquifers and rivers which stored water are used up.

The situation in those two vast nations, comprising about a third of mankind, is made worse by the global warming which is melting the reserves of water previously stored in the Himalayas, mountains which are the source of all the great rivers of India and China. This is exacerbated by the increasing demand for hydro-electric power and huge irrigation projects. With present trends, many predict that the wars of the future will be over water supplies and that scorched farm fields and desertification loom.

This is turning into a depressing catalogue of future disasters so I shall not go into other very serious problems – urban pollution which is afflicting many cities from Beijing to Kathmandu, the poisoning of the rivers with industrial effluent, noise and light pollution which damages the lives of many.

Instead I will end the outline of where we are now with noting the greatest threat of all, the one which some deny is happening, or if they concede it is present, deny that it is related to human activity, namely global warming.

The general principles are now roughly understood. The emission of 'greenhouse gases', that is certain elements which form a kind of 'greenhouse' or glass roof over the earth and stop accumulated heat from escaping, has been warming the planet rapidly over the last half-century. Many of these gases come from farming – particularly cattle for meat and milk – but the greatest comes from factories, transport and the burning of coal for energy. The result is that almost all of the hottest years in history have occurred in the last twenty years.

Measurements of the melting of the polar ice caps show that at both poles, vast amounts of hitherto frozen water and ice covered land, is unfreezing and even the permafrost across the belt across Russia and North America is unfreezing to allow increasing amounts of the dangerous greenhouse gas, methane, to escape.

It is predicted that, within the next generation, sea levels will rise to cover many low-lying islands and coastal districts. There may be other wider effects on the great ocean currents, for example shifting the Gulf Stream or altering El Nino. The likelihood of extreme climatic events – hurricanes, droughts, floods – is increasing.

I will not go into more of the details, most of which are generally known and the stuff of climate conferences. Standing back we can see that although Malthus was thinking within an agricultural world, where energy sources were obviously finite, since animals, wind, water and plants could, without a huge change technology, only produce a gradually increasing return, we are still trapped in a finite world. Unless we migrate in large numbers to other planets we seem to be heading towards the crises which he predicted – war, famine and disease.

*   *   *

Yet people point out that Malthus and Adam Smith predicted the limits to growth and an inescapable trap at precisely the moment when, in fact, new knowledge and machines, were, for a couple of centuries at least, able to raise the threshold of disaster. These two founders of modern economics could not with their laws and tendencies have imagined a world two hundred years later with ten times the population but where at least three quarters of the world population are above absolute poverty. Edward Gibbon estimated that three quarters of the world's population at that time were in misery – afflicted by poverty and war. Now, with ten times as many, three quarters have partially escaped from those disasters, at least temporarily.

In Smith's day, the top one percent lived a reasonably comfortable life of leisure, ample food, clothing and health. Now, more than twenty percent of a world population ten times that size, in other words well over 200 times as many people, live decently. So it is clear that it is difficult to suggest what will happen. What we can do, however, is to guess some useful ways of avoiding catastrophe.

*   *   *

The first concerns population control. It is clear that, at some point, population growth on this planet has to be restrained.

If we continue at present rates, within a few hundred years the human mass will be expanding outwards through space at thousands of miles a year. Whether we are content with the hoped for nine to twelve billion in the middle of the twenty-first century, or some higher figure another generation on, it is obvious that either through control of fertility, or through the Malthusian positive checks, population will shortly be halted.

Two things are needed if levelling is to occur. The first is that contraception, hopefully much improved, can be made available without stigma and very cheaply or freely to all on this planet who want it. The second is that religious or family systems which still encourage very large families, or forbid contraception, need to be challenged.

As we know, two of the most powerful religious-cum-family systems in the world, Roman Catholic and Islamic, are opposed to all family limitation. Yet things are changing as the reality of the connection between population, poverty and the miserable life of women becomes ever more obvious. The rising status of women, and in particular their ability to continue in education and to have a career, is having a huge effect. The wider effect of the consumer society and structural changes in such things as pensions and the perceived effects of a decline in infant mortality rates are other factors.

So it is not beyond hope that, when people look back in two generations, they will indeed see that population stopped galloping upwards sometime in the twenty-first century, even though at present we have a huge momentum with a very young world population entering the reproductive phase and often feeling that it is their duty, as well as to their private economic and social well-being, to have many children.

* * *

The second area to consider is how we produce energy. If anyone had predicted a generation ago that China would become the greatest producer of renewable energy products by 2016 it would have sounded incredible. It would at that time also have also seemed impossible that Germany is now producing all its energy without using coal, or that Britain now produces a quarter of its energy from renewable sources.

What is happening is that a mixture of a deeper understanding of scientific possibilities, combined with market pressures, is making it possible to envisage a future with much better batteries, much better distribution systems, much greater use of solar, wind and water power, and perhaps the longed-for major breakthrough. Such a breakthrough would be the discovery of a simple, effective, cheap, and non-polluting energy source such as fusion energy, or adapting the new miracle materials such as graphene. Such a breakthrough, could suddenly allow us to imagine a world with limitless, nonpolluting, renewable energy which can be distributed more or less freely, perhaps using effective superconductivity.

At a stroke, this would alleviate many of the other problems. The urban pollution by cars, the horrors of factory farming of animals, the destruction of forests, the shortage of fresh water, all these could be mitigated or avoided, if there was limitless, almost free, and non-destructive energy.

Just as someone looking back from the present is amazed at what coal and oil have done to lighten the load of human labour and to alleviate so much other misery, so, perhaps, in a hundred years if someone reads this they will say the same.

They may well ask - 'Was it not obvious to Macfarlane as he wrote this gloomy account that things were already changing? Did he not remember that Adam Smith was not aware of the implications of what was happening down the corridors in Glasgow University as James Watt was constructing a machine efficiently to convert coal into power through steam and machinery? Did Macfarlane not realise that, in the same way, in the ring of high tech and biotech science companies round Cambridge University, the silicone fen of East Anglia, small firms were inventing technologies which would soon be generalised and provide the basis for a new industrial revolution? This revolution would give humans an infinitely expanded set of new possibilities.'

In fact, this revolution is obviously already upon us and I have met and interviewed some of those who are already experimenting with the light receiving and emitting diodes, or the superconductivity systems, which will quite soon reshape our potential resources.

* * *

Yet technology alone, without population control as we have seen, only puts off the evil day without a change in attitudes to our wider environment and ecology. For one of our inherited problems, as economists and ecologists have pointed out, is to do with how we think of what is around us – the land, seas, forests, mountains and air.

Traditionally, most civilisations have divided the world into private property, protected in the interests of the owner, and public or 'common' property. This has led to the 'tragedy of the commons' as it is called, whereby public spaces are open to exploitation by all. There is little cost and often great benefits in exploiting these common resources. It is in people's private interest to pour industrial waste into rivers, to dump rubbish in the oceans, to belch out fumes from factories, farms and car exhausts into the atmosphere, to scoop up the fish or cut down the 'common' forests.

All this will continue until we recognise that there is no such thing as a 'free lunch'. All resources are, in fact, finite and in some sense, in this highly interconnected world, belong to us all. If Indonesia burns down its forests for palm oil, the neighbouring nations suffer terrible air pollution. If America fills its soil with chemicals and sand and releases huge amounts of carbon energy through fracking, all of us are affected. If Japan and China suck in the softwoods of Southeast Asia and the metals of Australia for their huge construction projects, it affect us all. If the Amazon is destroyed to produce hamburgers for McDonald's, all our lives are diminished.

'Ask not for whom the bell tolls - it tolls for thee'. In other words, we have to go through a mental and cultural revolution, which can only be achieved through political decisions, based on better education and explanation, whereby we look on all of the world's resources not as 'free-for-all' Commons, but held in trust for the future. We have to think of stewardship, and shared responsibility.

The model of 'Commons' in the English past, where a village would preserve its woods, waters, grazing and moors century after century by giving each household very strictly defined and limited rights and obligations could be extended. A system of quotas and limits, as has started to be effective in preserving fish stocks in the North Sea, is obviously the only way we can avoid wholesale destruction.

Often this runs into the law of 'free riding' pointed out long ago – namely that it is in a person's narrow self-interest to have three cars or go on many long-haul flights, or keep a large yacht, or a pack of dogs and cats, while each of these things contributes to the general diminution of mankind.

Whether we can, in time, learn how to share and steward our resources, is not certain. It has been done in the past, particularly when it becomes obvious that by forgoing their narrow and short-term gains, humans will benefit, as will their children and children's children. Casting your bread on the waters – eating less meat, economising on water and car journeys, seriously recycling, all these are small, personal, gestures, but they add up. They already make more sense to many who are increasingly aware that we live in a small, fragile, crowded, planet which is under huge pressure.

Our attitudes are changing, and often for the better. We cannot afford to despair and, with the leisure promised in a later chapter, we will have plenty of time to think about neat solutions to our apparently insurmountable, but ultimately soluble, difficulties.

TWO

Work and Machines

A CENTURY AND a half ago Karl Marx foretold the collapse of capitalism. The reason for the imminent socialist revolution was simple. Capital, that is money, machinery and the private ownership of all resources would become monopolised in a few hands. The working-classes would become redundant. Their labour would not be needed and they would be economi-cally powerless. They would rise in revolt and overthrow the capitalist system.

For one hundred years afterwards many people scoffed at Marx's prophecy. People seemed as busy as ever and the working-class seemed to increase its power through the Trade Unions and progressive legislation. It seemed a false prophecy. Yet it now seems that Marx may have been right, but for somewhat different reasons to those to do with the monopolization of capital that he put forward.

* * *

We can summarise the history of work and the rewards for labour briefly. Throughout almost all of human history since the advent of civilisation, the vast majority of the earth's inhabitants have had to work incredibly hard, while a small group of the literate and the militarily powerful have controlled them and lived in relative leisure. From slavery to serfdom to 'free' industrial and agricultural workers, people have had to use their shoulders, arms, legs and brains, harnessed to simple tools and to animals, to produce all the commodities they need for survival. This was the situation up to about one hundred and fifty years ago. Hard, physical, labour filled most of people's lives and it was a proportion of the fruits of that labour that sustained people.

What we have seen since then, as yet predominantly in the Western nations, but now very rapidly spreading around the world, is a stepped, but revolutionary, set of changes. I shall make the changes visual by illustrating them in terms of occupational groups who are represented by the nature (or absence) of the collars on their shirts. The colour of these collars is related to the degree of sweat involved in the job they are doing. I shall also illustrate the process mainly in relation to Britain and America, though it also happened in spreading ripples around the world.

In the second half of the nineteenth and first half of the twentieth century, the vast majority of people were agricultural workers, those who worked under the burning sun at tough farming tasks and often wore no collars at all. And in this precise century, in the West, they became redundant.

The process started with better agricultural machinery, ploughs and harvesting machines which meant that one person with horses could do the work of dozens. The fields emptied of labourers. This tendency grew ever more powerful with the advent of petrol and diesel driven tractors from the early twentieth century. These replaced the horses and increased the power of one individual so that he (and occasionally she) could do the work of several hundred labourers.

The vast expanses of North America, or the lesser fields of Europe, were finally emptied of a class of agricultural labourer who represented much of humanity's experience over the centuries. The same is happening today in India and China, with vast consequences. The high suicide rates among Indian farmers, the emptying of the countryside except for the old and the poor, the pouring of huge waves of migration into the expanding cities, these are all features of the shift from the countryside to the cities.

The second revolution occurred in the later half of the twentieth century, this time amongst those who also sweated, but perhaps to a lesser degree since they were working within buildings, the 'blue-collar' workers created by the first industrial revolution. Their work in mills, factories, workshops and mines, which had sustained them for nearly two centuries, was made unnecessary by a ratcheting up of the power of machinery. Almost all the goods previously dug out of the ground or manufactured with assembly lines could now be produced by ever more intelligent machines, so that again one person could do the work of hundreds. The dramatic closing of the factories and mines in the 1970's in Britain, and the rust belts of America, are the effects of the death of the blue-collar worker in the West.

For a while these blue-collar workers were partially replaced by similar, cheaper, workers in the East. But they too will soon be replaced. A machine can make most things that a human being can manufacture, at a fraction of the cost, and with far less friction in terms of labour relations. Future advances such as three-dimensional printers, which can manufacture, as they are needed, most items, from house and car parts to artificial human limbs, is just one of the current advances which will take this process even further. The day of the blue-collar worker is almost over.

The next group is those who work in 'offices', whether in centralised or distributed locations. They do not work principally with their bodies and hands (except transmitting ideas through a pen or keyboard) so they can wear white collars without fear of spoiling them. At one level they are the clerks, secretaries and lower administrators and bureaucrats of various kinds. Yet they also include the professional middle class, the doctors, lawyers, bankers, teachers, clergy, librarians and many other professional groups.

Hitherto this white-collar group has been protected by the fact that while it was not too difficult to invent tools for cutting hay or weaving cloth or fitting a wheel to a car, it seemed much more difficult to make tools with enough 'intelligence' to take the kind of decisions which white-collar workers had to make. This is all ending with the advent of increasingly powerful computers.

The computer is an 'analytical engine', as it was originally called, 'it computes' or works out solutions to questions. It can solve many kind of repetitive decision-making problem when fed with appropriate data and good programs. So the extraordinary rapid development of computing over the last half-century, which leads currently to a doubling in power of 'thinking machines' every nine months or so, means that computers can already probably do as well as humans in over three quarters of the tasks traditionally associated with white-collar work. Computers can diagnose illness, decide legal disputes, teach students to a reasonably high level, play the stock exchange, even drive cars and beat the best chess and 'Go' players in the world.

It seems obvious that people will look back on the first half of the twenty-first century as the period when almost all of the white-collar class were eliminated. One teacher, one lawyer, one doctor, plus machines will be able to do what one hundred do now.

All that will be left are those in some of the creative and service industries. Waiters, actors, musicians, painters and sportsmen will survive. As will what we may call the 'striped shirt' class. These are the very rich top executives in various bodies – the managers of universities, banks, hospitals – who are paid enormous amounts already and oversee increasingly few people and many machines.

All this will happen first in the 'advanced economies' of the United States, Japan and Europe. Yet China, India and other larger countries will join in the process very soon indeed.

So Marx's prophecy is likely to be fulfilled after all. Much manual and even intellectual work will be eliminated and done by machines. This will be in a world where there is a vast preponderance of young people coming into the labour force, and a world population of 7.4 billion which is still rapidly growing. What will happen in a world of ten billion, of whom 90% have no productive role?

* * *

There will be innumerable consequences, but here I will look at just three of them – the question of earning a living, the question of filling time, and the question of changing family relations.

During much of the recent past, particularly in market economies, but also in peasant societies, for most people wealth was derived from work. You grew crops, kept animals, worked in a shop or factory, and either used or sold what you produced, or earned wages working for others. So the whole modern system of allocation of wealth is derived from an economy which has been built up on the idea that in some sort of way, what you receive in cash or kind reflects your abilities and your labour. If this is undermined by the fact that human labour is hardly needed, except at the margins, what is to replace this system of allocation?

With unemployment running at ten or even twenty per cent, the Welfare State could hand out Social Security. But if unemployment is at ninety per cent, what then? Clearly this will not affect certain groups – the star footballers and entertainers, the top executives and bankers, who may continue to draw ever more gargantuan rewards. Nor will it affect some of the service sector. But what about the rest? How will the billions of young people in the future who have no job live, or even survive?

We have hardly begun to think about this, but there are a few experiments just starting. One is to separate work from income – as is done with Social Security – but on a universal basis. In other words to think of 'entitlements', not unlike the idea applied by Amartya Sen in relation to preventing famines. It would then be the 'entitlement' of every person living in a society, a human right if you like, not only to 'life, liberty and the pursuit of happiness' but also to enough income to make those things possible – guaranteed by the state.

Just as there is free healthcare and (mostly) free roads, there would be a certain minimum benefit or entitlement for everyone.

There are currently experiments, both with Social Security and in the more ambitious schemes to cover all citizens, envisage a 'living entitlement', set like a 'living wage', to make it possible for each adult and child to live a reasonable life – with enough food, clothing, housing, leisure spending.

This might, for example, in current circumstances, mean, depending on age, and the general state of the economy that each person received a guaranteed £2000 per month. The idea would be to set this level in order to make a reasonable living possible. Yet it would allow space, if a person wanted more, for them to have bi-occupations – to grow their own vegetables, keep chickens, set up a small service business, become an artist, writer, teacher, musician or professional sportsman, all of which would boost their income.

There are, no doubt, other and better ways to deal with a world where almost everyone, except those in the service industries and the top executives and sports persons, has no work. What is important, is that we need a radical rethink of the whole structure which has grown up over thousands of years of human labour.

We have to move, as Marx advised, beyond the capitalist model. Yet one thing we do know is that the experiment which Marx advocated as a solution, the abolition of private property and the state, fine as it might sound in theory, leads to disaster, to the horrors of Stalin, Mao and Pol Pot and now North Korea. That is not the solution – yet we need quickly to work out an alternative. 'Earning a living', in the sense that term was used in my earlier years, is almost dead.

* * *

The second consequence worth considering is – what will people do with their time? Through most of history, apart from the early years of infancy and education and a short retirement perhaps, most people's lives have been filled with work, interspersed with short periods of rest. Terrible though the toll has been, it did fill the days and sometimes the nights. Not only will that work be absent for most people, but with rapidly increasing longevity it will not just be a matter of filling the years to sixty or retirement, but to ninety or more.

If we use the distinction between work and leisure, then we are facing the problems foreseen by Thorstein Veblen in his *Theory of the Leisure Class* (1899). We are moving to a world where the lifestyles of country gentleman, Roman aristocrats, Russian nobleman, the tiny fraction of the wealthy and privileged in many societies is, in varying degrees, the life for all. This being so we can see part of the answer to the problem of filling time.

If we look at the lifestyle of those tiny elites in history who have not had to work, we find that they have often been able to fill their time with activities which gave their life enough pleasure and meaning. These can vary from creative and intellectual activities – arts, music, writing – to sports – hunting, shooting, fishing – to games of various kinds and to innumerable hobbies and interests.

All this could be encouraged and stimulated by an educational system which helps prepare people for a life of leisure. My own schooling, preparing me for a white-collar existence with a good deal of leisure, seemed to recognise this as did my university experience. Universities for centuries had taught the mind, but also how to appreciate leisure. Both at school and Oxford, I was encouraged to develop hobbies, interests, to write, enjoy poetry, paint, make things, participate in many sports and games.

My main emotional and social life was outside the formal 'work' training environment of the classroom. It was in the playground, the playing fields, the dormitories, on the stage and in the art room that my imagination and skills were most actively trained. My schooling and university training was about being taught skills and aesthetic tastes in order to enjoy nature, art, philosophy, and to learn the joys of creativity and the boundless enjoyment of working within my imagination. In other words our learning was about 'play' in the wider sense in which John Huizinga speaks in his book Homo Ludens (1938), arguing that the play instinct is one of our strongest drives.

If we are equipped with the knowledge and tools to explore our world in an imaginative, creative and playful way, there is more than enough to fill a life. The arrival of ever more powerful tools of leisure – television, computers, smartphones, alongside a world of virtual reality and online gaming, is already filling many peoples lives.

This can be observed in the massive expansion of the leisure activities of that new phenomenon, namely the 'third' and 'fourth' ages of man, stretching from retirement to the 90s. A large portion of the society in advanced countries is now aged over sixty. They are travelling, engaging in clubs and sports, teaching each other, filling up their time. As one friend joked to me on the point of retirement, envisaging the exhausting round of activities ahead, 'retirement is for a younger man'. It should not be beyond our abilities to plan for a world of leisure and play, once we recognise the vast change that is occurring.

* * *

There are numerous other consequences of the erosion or complete disappearance of conventional work, but here I will deal with only one more – namely the effect on family life.

The conventional life cycle in the Anglosphere was for the children to leave home either young, or at least at the end of formal education, and to go out to earn their own living in the wider society and economy. They could keep their own wages or set up their own business or work on their own farms, independent of their parents.

In the other type of family system to be found in the rest of the world, some at least of the children, probably the sons, would stay within the domestic unit, working with their family and, towards the end of their lives, supporting them. So they would work on the family farm or in the family firm and contribute to a joint stock of a kind – from which their sisters might draw their dowry and join another 'family firm'.

Both types of organisation are undermined if there is no traditional work to be done. How can children leave home to work for others and set up their own businesses or even buy a separate house if there is nothing to be done? If there are no jobs, they can only fall back on the one group who will probably feed and house them – their natal family. This is clearly happening on a large scale and means that for the first time in the Anglosphere, children are staying on at home into their late 20s and 30s.

We seem to be morphing into the kind of 'extended household' system which has never existed before in the Anglosphere. This goes against the whole tenor of the individualistic, equal, separate identity which has been built up over the last thousand years. Its consequences are hardly being discussed. How can a household have several, closely related, adults living together, particularly if the children are heavily dependent on their parents and grandparents to supplement their meagre or absent wages?

In the other world pattern, namely the domestic mode of production where the family acts together and stays together on the farm or the firm, the problem is different but just as great. There is no 'mode of production', domestic or otherwise, nothing for the children to contribute to. The unit becomes only one of consumption and perhaps some kind of joint ownership of the house property. Again this will put new strains and completely alter the nature of the family system.

At present in much of the Third World the loss of farming work has led to a huge wave of labour migration to the cities so that, for example in China, the children and grandparents are left in the villages. But this is again a temporary phase, for the very idea of 'labour migration' will vanish when the great factories of the east coast of China no longer need labour.

Here we do not have solutions. The best we can do at present is to be aware of the tendencies and trends, and to see if we can use our ingenuity to make new arrangements for this changing world. If we understand what is happening and is likely to happen, we can plan a little. Humans have adapted to the move from hunter-gatherer to tribal to peasant to capitalist. We should be able to construct a meaningful and fairer world without work for most. But we will only do so if we face the reality of what is happening. The problems that are looming have little to do with human evil, Chinese or Indian cheap labour, though those may be factors. They are largely to do with the replacement of human power by applied knowledge in the form of machinery.

THREE

Health and Longevity

F OR ALMOST ALL of history, humans, like other animals, were a rather defenceless prey for numerous pathogens, whether through vectors like mosquitoes, or the various bacteria and viruses which people could not see. Consequently, from one point of view, human history until about one hundred and fifty years ago could be written as a long and usually unsuccessful struggle against pain and death.

Many societies are still what anthropologists call 'disease-logged'. Having lived in such a society in Nepal, where initially there were practically no doctors, dentists or medicines, and almost everyone was suffering from some sort of pain almost all the time, I realise how fortunate many of us now are, who live in the prosperous parts of the world which have good medical facilities.

There were, of course, in many civilisations, traditional medicines and people often hit on environmental solutions which had very large effects – boiling water, reasonable housing, clothing and shoes, the drinking of tea and beer, which lowered the toll of various diseases. Yet without being able to understand the causes of disease, and without the possibility of devising powerful anti-bacterial and anti-viral protections, most of life was precarious.

The most vulnerable period was at birth, and in the first year. In many traditional societies people lost up to a quarter or more of their infants, as well as many mothers. If it were possible to survive to ten years old, there might be a good chance, in the absence of serious incidence of the great killers like smallpox, cholera, plague, tuberculosis, influenza, or malaria, to survive into one's fifties or even sixties. But then, with weakened bodies from heavy toil and no effective cures, even a minor illness could cause death, so that many people died in their sixties or seventies.

In such a situation, there was really very little that doctors could do, for they knew little more than did ordinary people, and there was really no point in institutions such as hospitals, which usually killed more people than they cured.

Three revolutionary developments in the hundred years from the middle of the nineteenth century changed all this, and a fourth current revolution is extending those changes.

* * *

The first huge change is in accurate knowledge. The story of the discovery of bacteria by the use of microscopes by Pasteur and Koch, and soon of the causes of malaria, bubonic plague, TB, cholera and other dreadful killers is well known and does not need to be rehearsed here. By the start of the First World War, much of disease causation had been mapped out. Yet it was not until the antibiotic and vaccination revolutions from the 1930s that the new knowledge could be applied through a wave of new medicines.

These two revolutions combined with a third, which was the

growth of a trained medical profession centred on hospitals. After the public health reforms of Chadwick and others, and the discoveries of disinfectants by Lister, hospitals could become places for healing rather than killing. So an era began when health care was institutionalised and the medical model for referring people to specialists and clinics and hospitals began.

The current and last revolution starts with the discovery of DNA by Crick and Watson in 1953 and the subsequent mapping of the human genome. Precision genetic manipulation, using techniques of replacing faulty DNA, along with other great breakthroughs like monoclonal antibodies, stem cell research, three-dimensional imaging, means that we are currently going through another medical revolution.

Of course, it is a war against sickness which can never be decisively won for several reasons. One is that bacteria, viruses, prions and other microscopic forms can mutate faster than humans and each generation of drugs soon becomes ineffective. Another is that death cannot, as yet, be put off for ever and the nature of the killers shifts from the traditional diseases to new, age-related ones, like dementia, Parkinson's, various cancers, heart attacks and strokes.

Furthermore new medical problems such as diabetes and obesity, new remote diseases like Ebola, new forms such as AIDS, are constantly changing and challenging our ability to bring more health and avoid disaster.

Yet things have changed and now in the more privileged parts of the world and particularly in the richer segments there, an infant can expect to live into his or her nineties, whereas (largely influenced by the high infant mortality) in most of the past and still in many parts of the world, the expectation of life at birth is a third of that.

All this may be counted as a blessing and we have come to expect pain alleviation, if not cure, as a human entitlement. We have also come to realise that the vast proportion of diseases and the high continued death rates in much of the world are preventable, not so much by hospitals and doctors but by good food, clean water and a cleaner environment.

* * *

What is not so often realised is that, as always, as we solve one problem it generates others. An obvious one comes under the heading of the revolution of rising expectations. We expect to live longer and to be cured and put pressure on our governments to facilitate this. This is combined with a population where there are many people living into their eighties and nineties.

Previously, through most of history, the population pyramid of most societies showed almost everyone being in the First and Second Age (childhood and work), with a few lingering over into the sixties and seventies. Now we have a situation, which is accelerating, where we have seen a change to the four ages of man (childhood and education; work; independent retirement; dependency).

Demographers and economists who have pointed to this very recent phenomenon have often warned us of the dangers of ageing populations, as in most of Europe, Japan, America and now in China. Yet their arguments are weak.

They worry that the young will not, through their labour,

be able to support a growing 'burden' of old people over the conventional age of retirement and consequently there will be a collapse of the economy. This argument is mistaken for at least two reasons. First is that it is derived from a previous, labour-intensive (farming and factory) economy where indeed, after the late 50s, the body could do less and people retired. We have moved away from such a world, as I explained earlier, to a knowledge, machine, service economy. The seventy or even eight-year-old with a computer can do just as much good 'work', as a person in their forties. It is a matter of expectations and organisation.

The second, connected, fact is that there is less and less of the old style work to be done – as shown above. The problem is leisure and how to fill it. The old-age-heavy pyramid we now have is no threat to this. If we add to this the potential improvement in health provision which means that those in the third age can keep fit and well, then this is a false worry.

Yet there is another consequence which requires much more thought and has hardly been addressed, what we might call the 'health-bucket-with-a-hole-in-it' syndrome. Let me explain.

* * *

The current health service in Western countries was built up from the middle of the 19th century on a model based on other institutional structures. Faced with the problem of mass education, you put people into schools and universities where they were taught from the front by teachers. Faced with the problem of spreading religious truths, there was a similar approach, with churches and ministers. With law it was the same, a court building, lawyers and judges. With producing goods, again there were the factories, the foreman and managers. The general aim was to achieve efficiencies and economies of scale by herding people into buildings, with one or two to guard or instruct them.

This worked reasonably well for a while and in the case of health, was coupled as the economies grew, with the provision of health care, either for free or through insurance, for most of the population. Healthcare became a vast, institutionalised, business. Yet we are all aware that the system is collapsing.

Hospitals are running out of money, doctors and nurses are overworked, people are dissatisfied. It is obvious why this is the case – it is due to the fact that health, including mental health and social problems, are based on needs that are infinite. This is especially so when we remember that the doctors, clinics and hospitals are also, for many, especially the retired, a way of passing the time and a chance for human company and conversation in our often lonely world.

So, like population, unless checked the number of patients grows exponentially. As Ivan Illich long ago argued, through their diagnosis and their need for patients and the money to be made from making and selling drugs, doctors and pharmaceutical companies create patients, in the same way as police create criminals, teachers create pupils, missionaries create sinners and intelligence services create terrorists.

Yet there is, as the population ages and new medicines and treatments are available, an ever-expanding perceived need. What can be done to deal with this? Here I will discuss three approaches, two of which seem to me to be useless, and the third a possible way forward, not just for the affluent societies of the West or the richest in India and China but also in what used to be called the Third World where per capita income is still less than one tenth of what it is in America or Britain. There, and increasingly even with the richest countries, it is not possible to use vast resources to help institutions.

* * *

The first approach, advocated by most politicians partly because it wins votes especially from the old, and obviously by the health lobby of manufacturers of medicines, is to spend more money. Increase the health budget at well above the rate of inflation or GDP growth, build more hospitals, buy more ambulances and expensive equipment, recruit and train more doctors and nurses, increase the budgets for ever more expensive medicines, provide more and more care to keep people alive as long as possible. The same argument is used by every group – more money for the exponential road network needed for cars, for universities for everyone, for a larger and better equipped police or Armed Forces. Yet few of these other needs touch everyone in their daily living in a way that health and sickness do, so they often have less influence.

In all cases, but particularly with the health system, seldom do such politicians or the lobbying groups stand back and ask when will it end? For it is obvious that if we spent the whole national budget on health – closing schools, shutting down all the social services, winding up the army and foreign aid, it would still not be enough. People would still be ill, drugs would still be getting more expensive, hospitals would still be stuffed with people who wanted treatment, doctors and nurses still over-worked. Thus more money without thought is useless – it is no longer the way, if it ever was.

* * *

A second approach which has been tried to make the health service more efficient is to treat it as a business, a factory, which produces things. Thinking of it as such a factory, sick people come in on a conveyor belt and move along it and are ejected as 'cured'. If this is so then surely the apparently effective management and production line methods that revolutionised American business in the twentieth century can be applied? This leads one towards management.

The way to deal with the problems is to take power and decisions away from the people who give the care – doctors and nurses – and hand it to management consultants. The same model is applied to schools, universities, the law, prisons and all the other institutions inherited from the nineteenth century.

In all these cases, there will, it is argued, be a double benefit. We can look at this with health. The doctors and nurses no longer have to divide their time between administering and healing, but can concentrate on the healing side where they are qualified. It will lead to greater efficiency gains because such doctors and nurses were never trained in business schools to run an organisation – so they do not know the jargon, the way to produce forms and transparency. Running something like a company or factory has to be taught in a serious course, so the top of each hospital should have a thick wedge of 'managers', very well paid, obviously, since it is such a responsible and difficult job. Since they control the wage bargaining, they can ensure that their expertise is suitably rewarded. The same is true of Vice Chancellors, Principals of big schools etc.

This business model was the favourite from the 1980s onwards, combined with the idea that doctors needed to be trained for longer and longer (a specialist will not attain his or her full licence until the mid or late thirties), nurses have to have degrees at universities and so on.

Alongside this it was the idea that public institutions are inefficient and perhaps if the services could be privatised then there would be big cost savings. The new administrators as well as the 'third way' politicians liked the idea of private-public partnerships. They also liked the idea of borrowing huge sums from the future by Private Funding Initiatives which would not start to cripple institutions until they had moved on.

We know what happened. People who knew little about health made the decisions, the doctors and nurses found themselves spending more time on administration than before as they serviced the administrators, there was a loss of commitment and involvement by the health staff, the administrators decided on ineffective and very expensive schemes (computerised records etc), competition about league tables and efficiency targets, obsession with budgets and transparency rather than alleviating sickness absorbed most of the energy. In other words, what happened in all of the professions at this time – the law, police, universities, schools – where administrators were introduced and the institutions became more inefficient and costly, occurred in health. So this does not seem to be the solution.

* * *

What is the alternative? Let me first suggest a few of the models and ingredients which seem part of the prescription. One is derived from the experience of the civilisation which has the longest continuous development of health care in a vast population in the world, namely China. The Chinese population has traditionally been remarkably healthy and has given to the West many of the medicines and techniques which relieve much pain – tea, ginseng, rhubarb and, recently, a new class of anti-malarials based on Artemisia. Along with acupuncture and many other traditional cures and medicines for colds, cuts, bruises stomach and other complaints, which, from my own experience, seem to work effectively, the Chinese have built up a large, non-hospitalised, medical system.

China has a huge population and was per capita not wealthy enough to set up a western style institutional healthcare system. Nor did it have the institutional tradition of large residential buildings with experts. Such a system of 'asylums', in schools, universities, prisons, churches, were only really introduced by missionaries and other Westerners. So when it came to dealing with the health crisis after the devastation of the Sino-Japanese war and the Civil War, when the Communist Party came to power in 1949, the move was not towards hospitals or highly trained doctors which would, in any case, not have not been affordable. As in other experimental places such as Cuba, the approach was informal, local and practical – in China widely known as the 'barefoot doctor'.

This meant that, after a very short medical training in basic health care, being paid very little, peripatetic and carrying only basic medicines, millions of health workers went across a country where three quarters of a billion people lived and brought healthcare to the remotest villages and the densest of cities.

It seems that, as I have observed, in the face of an increasing demand and a huge population, a modified version of this barefoot doctor scheme is being revived in China. In the experimental areas where it is being tried out, each small village has a little clinic, staffed by a lightly trained and modestly paid worker aided by voluntary or part-paid inhabitants – retired city-dwellers, retired nurses and doctors – who help with diagnosis and prescribing for 90% of the problems which occur at the village level and can be dealt with there. They have the time, the local knowledge and may live locally, so they can deal with the needs for assurance and conversation which takes most people to doctors surgeries and pharmacies.

Only in the ten percent of cases where the symptoms look serious and they do not know what is wrong, are patients referred to a small local hospital in the local town. This institution can then filter out, with simple equipment and lower-level doctors, another ninety percent of those referred. This leaves only one percent of all the people who originally come for healthcare to be sent on to major, specialist, hospitals for difficult diagnosis and treatment. This is a model for India, Africa, South America and elsewhere.

* * *

If we take this story to more affluent, as yet, Western societies like Britain we can add to it two further recent changes. The first is the effect of the Internet. It is obvious that there is a vast, and often very high quality, amount of information about most diseases and symptoms available on a number of web-sites. Many people now consult Wikipedia or particular health websites when they have a symptom and then either go to the pharmacy, or take their self-diagnosis print-out to the GP for checking and confirmation.

This is just the start of a revolution in self-healing, which, with encouragement and some guidance, could expand. It is infinitely cheaper, more personalised, and probably better in delivering all round health than our inherited system based on highly trained and paid professionals in expensive buildings, with hugely expensive equipment and medicines.

The second element is the frequently mentioned feature of leisure in the third and fourth ages. I know that in my small fen-land village near Cambridge there are a dozen or more retired or semi-retired individuals, or spouses, or others who already have the skills, perhaps as retired doctors or nurses or paramed-ics, or who can easily be trained to a reasonable level in a short time, to deal with much of the burden of milder sickness. This kind of localised approach has long been practiced in the fields of local government, law and the church, with magistrates, church helpers, parish councilors, working for free and for the interest and as a contribution to the society. 'Village Colleges', to which my children and grandchildren went up to the age of sixteen, are another part of this localisation process.

In other words, what could be created is a kind of 'Neigh-bourhood Health' system, a term derived from the self-polic-ing movement of 'Neighbourhood Watch', where people liv-ing nearby taken on amateur policing functions. So we could develop a system where each community, parish, part of a city, would look after most of its own health problems in very local small clinics and with easy visiting of the sick or needy. A small supply of resources, encouragement and mentoring could work wonders - and if problems of confidentiality emerged, there could be a system of people working in nearby, but not personally known, villages or districts.

Obviously such a solution could apply not only to physical sickness, but also to all those other related problems, mental health, delinquency, loneliness, disability. This would not only be far cheaper and more effective, but, returning to the idea of civil society, it would strengthen community identity, self-government, 'health' in the wider sense.

Again I have seen the beginnings of this in my little village where a recently, built, small community hall, used for meetings, leisure, elections and now even with a small piece of medical equipment (to be used in case of cardiac arrest), could also easily be a health centre. It is next to the village playing-field, the children's play area, the church, graveyard, village vegetable allotments, and the local post-office and shop. This returning of many aspects of life to the localities, including healing, could be a really significant development far beyond the health role.

It may all sound, once again, idealistic, utopian, unrealistic. It will face many vested interests and older conventional ways of thinking. It will need to be tested and adapted for different cultures, for what works in China will not easily work in the West and vice versa. Yet if we do not think in a radical way as our world changes dramatically, we are just marching into an ever-narrowing valley which will finally trap us. We should think in new ways to fit a world of increasing expectations and technology, but also increasing leisure and information. China is already leading the way, though it has also partly caught the 'hospitalisation' disease. So it may be that once again, as with printing, compasses, paper, porcelain, gunpowder, let alone tea and rhubarb, we can learn from the Chinese.

FOUR

Democracy and Civil Society

T HERE HAVE BEEN numerous schemes and dreams of how best to govern human societies. Amongst these are aristocracy (rule by the best) plutocracy (rule by the richest) oligarchy (rule by the few) autocracy (rule by an absolute leader) kleptocracy (rule by thieves) bureaucracy (rule by officeholders) communism (rule by the Party), republican (rule by ordinary individuals), monarchy (rule by a king) and democracy (rule by the people). Each has its advantages and disadvantages. If we take a very rapid tour through some of them we can see where we now are and the possible paths ahead.

Hunter-gatherer societies, which dominated the planet for most of human history, had no instituted rulers. Individuals decided for themselves what they would do, though they might pay attention to an older and more experienced member. He or she had no way of enforcing his will but might persuade a small group to follow.

With the domestication of animals and plants leading into tribal societies, it was possible for people to become temporarily richer and more powerful during their lives, so they are called 'Big Men' societies. There might be chiefs or elders who could exercise some control, largely through distributing wealth to their followers. They were self-made and only marginally different from commoners or small men (and women).

When civilisations emerged around ten thousand years ago, instituted stratification and government became possible and the era of divine or semi-divine rulers emerged. In the ancient civilisations of the Middle East, the Indus Valley and the Yellow River, there arose absolutist rulers, Pharaohs, Emperors, Kings, who directed armies, raised taxes and acted as mediators to the gods. This form of absolutist government, with the rulers lifted on to another plane, what nowadays might be termed despotism, or in its milder form absolutism, has re-emerged from time to time through history in new guises. It can be found in the absolutist monarchies of the eighteenth century in Europe, or the Communist and Fascist regimes of the twentieth.

A little under three thousand years ago some of the small city states in the Greek peninsula, in particular Athens, experimented with a new form of governmental system, rule by (some of) the ordinary people or 'democracy'. The cities were by our standards small and the proportion of those eligible to vote also small. In Athens, a city reckoned to be between 250 and 300 thousand at its peak, only free male property holders, between thirty and fifty thousand at the most, were politically active. Excluding women, slaves and the poor, this was about one in ten. They could participate, listen to speeches and arguments, and take part in making decisions about how to proceed.

This ideal of a meeting place, Agora, where people argued in public in oral debate has been an inspiration ever since. It was partially adopted into Roman government during the early, Republican ('Res Publica' - public things), phase of the Roman

Rule. The Republic was overthrown after several centuries and Rome moved to an Imperial, absolutist, rule.

Meanwhile, in China, the Qin Emperor in 221 B.C. unified China and started to institute a system that has dominated that vast empire since – rule by an educated elite of civil servants, a bureaucracy based on examination success, experts who advised and ruled as Mandarins under an Emperor who held Heaven's Mandate.

Another main form of rule, which we call feudalism, is where power is devolved down a chain of contractual agreements of service and protection. The King or most powerful warlord devolves land and power down to his nobles, and they do the same to inferior lords and so on down to ordinary people. This system emerged in the West in the thousand years after the fall of Rome from the fifth century A.D., and in Japan from about the 12th century.

Hence there were various sub-units, the Lords in their manors, the merchants and manufacturers in their towns, the monks in their monasteries, the teachers in their universities, each of which had a great deal of control over their own lives. There were numerous strong bodies or corporations in which the individual could find protection, what we term 'civil society'.

Another system was implemented by Mohammed and instituted in Islam, where power of a military, religious and political kind was unified into the hands of one or two individuals. Yet it was not highly centralised since great stress was placed on individualism, equality and contract. Primary allegiance was to Allah. There was little civil society as all forms of grouping – cities, churches, universities, kinship and economic groupings – were given little or no power and sharia law did not recognise more than the very simplest of corporations. Yet it was not a highly centralised, absolutist, system either so that it fitted with none of the other four categories of imperial, feudal, bureaucratic or democratic rule.

span of control to key

* * *

Through the last 500 years in the West, some of the smaller entities, nations or city-states, preserved and even expanded the idea of democracy. The Italian city-states such as Florence, Venice and Sienna, had a large measure of self-government with many male inhabitants playing a part in ruling themselves. The same happened with the Dutch from the middle of the sixteenth century. The same was the preserved tradition in England.

Aiken

The roots of modern democracy are widely acknowledged to lie in the peculiar system that grew up from Anglo-Saxon roots in the sixth century onwards, through the medieval parliaments, the contests of Crown and Parliament in the seventeenth century down to the constitutional monarchy where Parliament is sovereign today. Of course, for almost all of this period, 'democracy' consisted of males who were relatively independent property holders, that is to say, as in Greece, perhaps about one in ten of the population.

Yet the electorate was gradually extended in the nineteenth century and the first half of the twentieth century to include all adults. In the United States all of the population, including Blacks, were not given votes until the 1960's.

Alongside the formal Parliamentary system there was an enormously powerful system of civil society institutions. From the local government run by parishes and county agencies, the powerful vested interest groups of lawyers, clergy, merchants, down to numerous clubs, pubs and organisations, people ran much of their own lives. The law was based on widespread participation in self-government through the juries and attendance at courts and taking on local offices such as constables. Most people in England from the late medieval period in England had a large measure of self-government. This was the system which was taken to America.

The system worked reasonably well in its restricted, semi-democratic, way in a Britain with around forty million, almost exclusively white, inhabitants by the First World War. It also worked in the thinly populated United States with about 100 million inhabitants at the start of the First World War. People could feel in control of their own lives, making the decisions which affect them in much of the Anglosphere, even to a certain extent in the non-white part of the British Empire, especially India. The ideal of rule of the people, by the people, for the people, was, it seemed, the noble outcome of the Greek inheritance.

* * *

Such a system was not without its enemies. On the right, that is where there is centralisation of power into the hands of one or a few individuals, the absolutist monarchies of the eighteenth century throughout most of Europe and Russia, followed by the Napoleonic conquests, threatened the system. Later the threat was resurrected when all of the western part of the European continent became Fascist only two generations ago. Fascism means 'bundling together', the destruction of all lower sources of power, all civil society or elective democracy. All devolved power is bundled back into a centralised power held by a small group of absolute rulers.

The other challenge was from the left, where, inspired by Marx's ideas that the miseries of mankind were caused by private property and hence inequality and the capitalist system which controlled the State, so that the cure would be communism – a return to communes or communities. This was a dream of universal freedom, sharing, equality, the end of alienation and repression. It was immensely attractive.

The tragedy was that eliminating private property and the State did not eliminate the need to have a system of power and control, or some method to allocate resources in the absence of a capitalist market. The nightmares of Stalinism, the Cultural Revolution and Pol Pot, the return to 'Year Zero' and mass extermination on a scale even greater than Hitler, was the result. Communism does not work. But many are now asking whether democracy, the rule of the people by the people is working either. Are the fears that mass democracy will lead to elective dictatorship coming about in the much larger and more impersonal worlds of the early twenty-first century?

The problem, at its simplest, is one of scale, to which is added many other pressures. The feeling that your vote counts made some sense when a few thousand or even 100,000 chose a member of Parliament or a member of the House of Representatives. One might know, or was able to visit, one's representative, lobby them and receive replies to one's letters. So it made sense up to roughly the First World War. It also made sense when we knew only a limited amount about the machinations of those who had been elected. With the full exposure of television and other modern media, with a more general undermining of respect for authority, the feet of clay are all too visible.

When we are faced with the diversity of modern Britain, with over sixty million inhabitants, or even more so the United States with 320 million, let alone the thought of introducing democracy into China with 1.4 billion or creating a real democracy in India with a similar population, how can it work? And how, even if it works there, can it be introduced into the many parts of Africa, South America, Pakistan or elsewhere, which face manifold problems of poverty, endemic corruption, sectarian violence, high illiteracy and poor education, and little tradition of civil society?

Democracy worked reasonably in eighteenth or nineteenth century Britain and America because they were relatively affluent, cohesive, peaceful and with vibrant local institutions and civil society. Yet, as we have seen with the recent attempts to force democracy at the point of a gun in Afghanistan, Iraq, Libya and elsewhere, it seems to be very inappropriate, as yet, in many parts of the world.

So we currently live in a world with many threads, systems and experiences from recorded history. Each system has its merits, but even democracy, as Winston Churchill put it, is the worst of all systems, except for all the rest which are even worse. Yet it is even questionable whether, in the present circumstances democracy, apart from being an ideal, is indeed the least bad of systems. It is not too difficult to argue that the sudden application of democracy to faction-filled places, most obviously the belt from Nigeria to Pakistan, has been a disaster.

* * *

It is perhaps not surprising that the largest Empire the world
has known, that is the British Empire, should have sought to
impose its own governmental system, based on that in a small
island, wherever it went – though with huge modifications when
it met large native populations who were largely excluded. Nor
is it perhaps surprising that when the so-called democracies of
the Anglosphere defeated the fascist regimes of Europe and
Japan, and successfully confronted the Communist regimes of
the Soviet Union and China, they should attempt to spread
their own governmental system as far and as fast as possible.
Democracy was equated with economic development, human
rights, education and freedom. So, especially after the collapse
of the Soviet alternative and the opening of China to market
capitalism, democracy seemed what the world needed and
within sight.

Yet many people can see that some alternative to historical democracy needs to be devised and that the same is true in
India and China. A system invented on a small island in western
Europe is not necessarily the solution for mankind. It is tempting to quote Alexander Pope: 'For forms of government let fools
contest. Whatever is best administered is best.' But before we
leave it at that, it is worth considering some possible paths from
where we are now to where we would like to be.

* * *

As we look back on the chaos and failures of the democracy
project of the last thirty years we may wonder what went wrong.
For an anthropologist familiar with cargo cults in Melanesia, it
looks as if the neoliberal democratic crusade was like the idea

held by certain remote tribesman. They had seen, or heard about, airplanes which landed and spilt out wonderful goods or 'cargo' at airports. The trick was obviously to build a landing strip and the planes would be attracted to them and unload their bonanza. The strips were built, in the same way as the ballot boxes and voting slips were distributed, and people waited. But neither the planes, nor recognisable democracy appeared.

The analogy reminds us that democracy, like laden planes, only works within a certain context. It will only work once you have a floor, an under-carpet and a ceiling to protect you from the elements. Just throwing the outer mechanisms of democracy, the ballot boxes and the assemblies, into societies with totally different histories, laws, customs and social structures is bound to lead to some pretty strange and contorted outcomes. We can see them all over the world, and particularly now in the Middle East, Africa and South America. Even in North America, democracy seems to be being derailed in a presidential race which exposes the detachment of the mass of Americans from their political system.

* * *

So what can one recommend? Here, thinking principally of how China, with its huge population, could develop a system which best gives its citizens a feeling of participation and freedom, I will suggest four things – the rule of law, the power of civil society, the control of corruption, and the genius of scale. Let me elaborate on each of these briefly.

In its classical sense, the 'Rule of Law' means that the law is above all individuals and all are equally subject equally to it.

The private interests, factions and power hungry are accountable to the law. It also means that law is universally applicable to all – men and women, old and young, rich and poor, religious and ethnic groups.

In other parts of the idea, all are equal, with equal rights and freedoms, in the sight of the law. The judges are outside the political, economic, ideological control and can act as impartial umpires or referees. The individual has a right to be tried by his or her peers, that is by equals, and cannot be subjected to arbitrary arrest. All disputes must be settled by law and not by physical or other violence.

This sounds idealistic and it is certainly not easy to institute. China is trying to incorporate this 'rule of law' by various serious reforms today. We have to recognise that such a process can have serious implications for a one-party state where political power is dominant over all of life. For the rule of law means sharing power with non-party officials who are independent. Yet without such a system, democracy in the wider sense of imparting a sense of security, freedom, self-fulfillment and self-government is not possible.

Consequently, those who advocate the ends – democracy – must pay close attention to the means – the rule of law. Until there are independent judges, a uniform and universal law, individual rights and responsibilities, protection of the individual by juries which decide guilt and innocence, there cannot be the kind of democracy which many yearn for.

* * *

The second under-carpet is civil society. The state is strong and would like to control almost everything, the lone individual is weak and unable to stand up to it. Yet when individuals form into teams, associations, groupings with real power and independence from the state, then they become empowered. This is the wider meaning of democracy in Alexis de Tocqueville's sense.

Tocqueville was not concerned with ballot boxes in his account of English and American democracy, but with civil society or associationalism. He knew that if a country consists of thousands of independent subgroups – local government organisations, educational organisations, religious groupings, businesses, city authorities, clubs and trusts and many more, then power is shared. These associations give people a sense of participation, they train people in democratic skills, they mediate and, if necessary, oppose tendencies towards the monopolising power of the state. That is why they are hated and destroyed in the build-up to communism, fascism and within some of the more extreme Islamic states.

The presence of these numerous intermediary bodies is a constant undermining of the powerful state. This is why Thomas Hobbes in Leviathan advocated their abolition. Attempts to abolish the associations failed because they had become deeply embedded in the British legal system. Anglo-American law recognises that there can be bodies, corporations, which are set up by private individuals who join together in a common purpose, sinking some of their individual power into mutual support. Belonging to them gives satisfaction, protection and support.

If democracy is to flourish in India, China or South America, or to revive in North America or Britain, civil society, public and common activities, have to be encouraged. And it is essential that they are protected by an independent judiciary. The state will try to subvert them as a threat, so they need powerful defenders. As they grow they may become overweening, as in some huge international corporations, particularly in America, which are more powerful than most governments. Yet they should, within reason, thrive if we are to survive.

* * *

A third underpinning is the control of corruption. Corruption, in one dictionary definition, includes the ideas of 'impairing integrity, virtue, or moral principle... loss of purity'. It is the infiltration, poisoning, degrading, polluting of purity. In other words it means that a body is invaded by another body. At its simplest it is mostly used to describe where an ideal of separation is not held to.

Modernity consists of the separation of wealth, power, society and belief, but where this modernity is threatened then there is 'corruption'. Economic decisions are corrupted by using kinship connections. Political decisions are corrupted by economic lobbying. Economic decisions are corrupted by political power or religious ideologies. Academic integrity is corrupted by the use of influence or money. When the supposedly individualistic, meritocratic, equal and level playing field is secretly invaded by other actors with concealed powers, then we have corruption.

It takes many forms as we know. When the market, law or political system itself is highly inefficient, over-bureaucratic, or too weak or too strong, corruption may be the only way to get things done. Without the 'informal' or black economy, much of the world's formal economy would collapse. Without the 'connections' which dominate in much of the world there would be very little activity. So there are degrees, and even some necessity for, limited corruption in an imperfect world. Yet if the scale is too great or the nature too extreme, then it becomes dangerous and debilitating.

There are several known cures. One is to pay all key employees a decent, living, wage so that they do not have to dabble in forms of corruption. The police, teachers, government officials, judges and many more are usually paid so little, even in booming economies such as China or India today, that they have to spend much time and energy in trying to raise money through informal means. To solve this problem is a circular, bootstrapping, operation. In order to afford to pay decent salaries the state requires the money which can only be amassed when corruption is diminished. Where do you break into the circle?

The second cure is transparency and accountability. If corruption is regularly exposed by whistleblowers or the media and, when exposed, punished by the courts, it is a disincentive. This, again, is what the Chinese and many others are trying to do. But again, if taken to extremes, as in the American taxation system with its systematic erosion of trust and time wasting (and lawyer and accountant funding) forms, it is not effective. Ever greater regulation and prosecution undermines trust and adds to the friction of bureaucracy, of which many living in over-bureaucratic societies are aware. It also leads to a state of permanent anxiety and insecurity at the threat of anti-corruption drives, which are often used as political tools and are widespread now.

Nevertheless, once we have recognised that corruption is not an isolated evil, or even something inherently criminal, innate in human psychology, but is due to a systematic set of arrangements – a poorly integrated market, the underpayment of officials, the lack of trust, the weakness of law, over-bureaucratisation, then we can do something about it.

* * *

Finally there is the 'Genius of Scale' which has been used to describe Cambridge and its Collegiate system. Human beings work best and feel happiest if they belong to a community of just a few dozen or a few hundred people. Humans evolved in small bands and feel in control and involved when we know each other personally. The 'imagined community' of vast nation-states or Empires is difficult to identify with.

The problem is that organisations get bigger, as do states. For example Cambridge University was perhaps ten times as big at the end of the 20th century as it had been a century before. Yet because of the college system, where new 'communities' could be created by a number of new colleges in the second half of the 20th century, Cambridge could retain its feelings of intimacy and community. The same is true of many organisations; regiments in an army; houses in a boarding school; departments in a business organisation; sporting or other clubs. There can be many of them, often in simulated opposition, each has a strong sense of identity and belonging and self-government.

If we extend this idea to the problem we face with building democracy and self-government in the agglomerates of the United States, India, China or even Britain, we can see that the more we can foster sub-groupings with an identity, the more people will feel a sense of shared purpose and self-control. This overlaps with, but is not the same as civil society. This also links to the final idea on how to govern the huge nations which have emerged, whose size has put so much strain on conventional participatory democracy.

This is the idea taken from Adam Smith related to the function of the state. His ideas might be encapsulated also in the idea of the genius of scale in another form – namely that decisions should be taken at different levels by those who are affected by them, or their delegates, according to their scale.

This has long been the tradition in Britain where decisions were localised. The church decided how to mend the parish roof or bell, the parish council decided on the footpath and the lighting. The manorial courts decided many small economic and legal matters. Yet things at a higher level, involving a whole county, were decided by county level bodies, the justices, the country gentry and others, and so on upwards to Parliament. The same is true in the federal United States.

Finally the State would only deal with those matters which concern all the inhabitants, for example the defence of the whole country, relations with other independent countries, very large infrastructural projects, national laws. It would act as a 'night watchman' does in the factory – not interfering with the ordinary machinery and people, but making sure that there were no fires or burglaries.

Something like this obviously exists in all huge agglomerations of the federal kind, whether the United States, India or China. There is a tendency, as is reported of China, for the state to exist in a top-down manner where, while in theory delegating power to lower levels, in fact almost all decisions, even at the lowest levels, have to be referred upwards for approval. We can see this pattern throughout Chinese history where, because of the top-down power structure and the insecure position of those at lower levels, it was essential to guard yourself against being accused of taking the wrong decision. It is still true that a local headmaster or other local official can be sacked, a talk cancelled or a newspaper shut down by the highest levels within the centralised Communist Party in a way that is more difficult, if not impossible, in the Anglosphere.

What is required is trust, and the apportionment of responsibilities to the appropriate level. Also needed is training and inducements to people to become involved in their own self-government, often as part of their un-paid civic duty. It does not come naturally or easily, but as with all the other paths, if we have some idea of where we are heading, what needs to be done, then we can, with Confucius, take the first step which may lead us on a long, and hopefully fruitful, journey.

Computers and Communications

H UMAN BEINGS, LIKE other animals, shape their world through the ways in which they communicate. Humans receive about seventy percent of the information they derive from the external world through their eyes and the rest through the other four senses. A brief overview of world communication systems will show that we live in an unprecedented revolution in terms of experiencing the world, which builds on, but exceeds that of all previous changes.

The first great change occurred about ten thousand years ago with the discovery of writing. The ability to inscribe ideas onto a solid medium – bone, stone, papyrus, wood, clay – had enormous effects. It made civilisations possible, it transformed economies with the notion of property, it made government much more powerful, raising taxes and able to send messages over long distances. It led to the rise of written religious and legal codes, clergy and lawyers. So we know that the world was changed radically by writing.

The second revolution occurred with the discovery of methods of reproducing or replicating written texts by the use of machines – what we call printing. First discovered in China around the eighth century A.D., printing with metal, movable, type was established in Europe by Gutenberg and his associates from the middle of the 15th century.

Those who have studied what is known as the 'Gutenberg Galaxy' have argued that as it developed in western Europe this type of printing had profound effects. Amongst those suggested are the birth of nationalism and the spread of national languages; religious schisms in the birth of Protestantism; the Scientific Revolution and the idea of progressive accumulation of knowledge and the correcting of earlier mistakes; the widening of education based on the multiplication of texts. Truth was now on the page, exterior to the individual, and people were united by books and increasingly newspapers in newly imagined communities. The period between the fifteenth and mid-nineteenth centuries were, in the West, the age of print.

The next revolution developed from the discovery of another machine, this time one which captured in a mechanical way what the eye saw – what has been termed 'the age of mechanical reproduction'. The discovery of photography in the earlier nineteenth century, and then of moving pictures at the end of century, transformed what people could observe, share and exchange. The world shrank with the photograph, and truth again was modified as it came to be represented by the camera which, some believed, never lied. Photo-journalism and the mass cinema were only two of the manifestations and vehicles for this.

Though it came along different paths, the discovery of the radio and then television in the late nineteenth and mid-twentieth century supplemented the power of photography and film. It is difficult to overestimate the effect of these two media in every part of life, from consumerism to sports and politics.

Again truth was given a new meaning as the world shrunk and expanded in new ways.

* * *

The final revolution is more difficult to write about because we are in the middle of it. It is sometimes called the Digital Age, sometimes the Internet Age, sometimes the Computer Age, sometimes a Multimedia World. What all these refer to is the ever increasing effect of the computer.

At first, when discovered by Charles Babbage in the first half of the nineteenth century, and then formally specified and instituted by Alan Turing and others in the middle of the twentieth century, it was not clear what the computer would do or how powerful a device humans had discovered when they invented a machine that appeared to think.

In the first thirty years of its widespread existence, that is between the 1960's and 1980's, it transformed business, government and transport, but it was still not clear how it would permeate every aspect of life from arts and education to war and law. Now, with the supplementary power of linking computers effectively – the Internet from 1992 – and miniaturisation and increasing power, as in smart phones, and it's harnessing to everything from drones to robots to surveillance cameras – it is becoming clear that we are living in a new age of instant communication across the globe. The remotest communities in the Himalayas or the Amazonian jungles, the poorest and the richest, young children and the elderly are all linked together in an unprecedented way.

We are only at the start of working out the implications of

this revolution. Popular applications such as MySpace, Facebook, Twitter, are less than fifteen years old and many more are no doubt being dreamt up. The most ambitious assemblies of human knowledge in history, huge digital libraries and encyclopedias such as the vast Wikipedia, have suddenly emerged. Much of the sum of human knowledge held in manuscripts, archives, books, photographs and films are now widely accessible, free and searchable with powerful tools such as Google.

Humans have never lived in such a world before, so it is difficult to work out the potentials, dangers and implications of the fourth great communications revolution. All that we know is that we are living through an age when the human brain is engaged in absorbing knowledge and expanding thought at an unprecedented speed. What implications does all this have for planning for the future?

* * *

My formal schooling for well over ten years almost exclusively trained me to survive in an age of written communication, the age of the journal and the book. I spent year after year of learning to read and write, to construct arguments with alphabetical letters, to appreciate great literature and to become, in my way, a critic. There were other symbolic systems which we also learnt, mathematics and to a certain extent music and art. Yet writing, combined with the content of English history and a great deal of Latin and some French, were the staples. All of this made sense in the 1950's and 1960's before what I shall call the computer age, but clearly it is not sufficient now.

Most people, including children, are gaining most of their

information about the world, apart from that from friends and family, by way of electronic media, that is television and computer screens including smart phones. So it is obvious that they should be being trained in three crucial life skills. One is how to 'read' these media, in a parallel way to learning to read books. Secondly they should be taught how to 'write' in these media in the way we were taught to write letters and essays. Thirdly they need to be taught how to handle the enormous and conflicting pressures of living in a world awash with digital information, which can so easily become compulsive, addictive and sometimes dangerous.

Let us take reading media, or, as the classic book by James Monaco calls it, How to Read a Film (1977 and later). What we see on screen, whether in the cinema, television, iPads or smart phones, is composed of complex arrays of colours and patterns, of sound and movement, an artificial and highly symbolic construct made by a mixture of humans and machines using advanced software (such as CGI). The messages we receive are based on rules and grammar in the same way as writing and the screens are filled with conventions, tricks and hidden power.

Because such communications are at one level so easy to read (even animals and babies can read simple films, while it takes years to read texts well), it is easy to assume that, unlike reading books, we do not need to learn how to read visual images. Yet if we do not seriously instruct people, preferably at school, but also at any age, in learning how to understand as well as to superficially 'read' the images presented to us, then we are trapped.

We need to learn how visual media works on us and shapes us without our being aware of it, to avoid being caught and manipulated in the way that George Orwell described in relation to writing in some of his essays. To avoid being at the mercy of powerful media barons, marketing interests and governments and pressure groups, we need to be able to discriminate truths from propaganda, lies from damned lies.

So every school should have serious classes where something equivalent to what we used to call 'muck-a-pre' (music appreciation) is taught with similar intensity to learning to read written texts. We need to learn the grammar, syntax, vocabulary and conventions of multiple media, computers and the Internet. Such training should be as well funded and privileged as the learning to read in the older ways.

* * *

When I learned to read, this was both aided and made more interesting by learning simultaneously to write. The two were inextricably bound together. The same is true of learning to survive in the computer or Internet Age.

It is not enough just passively to learn to read what is on the screen, we should be taught all the arts of 'writing' on them with these new formats as well. Although at the time it was often frustrating and exhausting, I had the good fortune to be working early in the process of this revolution.

Computers were very basic when we started to use them and we had to work closely with several generations of software engineers in Cambridge to develop our own database systems, query languages, our own early versions of HTML, the Internet and Google before any of these had been invented. This forced us to learn something about how computers worked, and the nature of programming. It is all much simpler now with packages and 'apps'. But all students should still learn enough of the basic language and structure of the computing world to enable them to live comfortably and safely explore in our Internet age.

* * *

The same good fortune applied to the development of my understanding of visual imagery. I first filmed before the advent of 'video', and when video arrived there were no powerful editing packages. So I had to construct my own methods, to learn from the bottom up, to teach myself how to film, how to edit and later how to share the films I made in the early days of the Internet.

Again, while avoiding some of the tedium of incredibly antiquated hardware and software, it does seem essential that all citizens should learn the basics of making films as a way of really understanding how they are being manipulated by media. They should be encouraged to share their products with others and have them criticised, and to learn the advantages and disadvantages of making them public on the cloud.

More generically, people should be given instruction on how the different media, single or in combination, affect us and can be best used. This should be a part of any modern training. Writing, photography, filming, television, social media, all work in different, if overlapping ways and should be understood at least in their basic principles. An introductory course which covers symbols and signs, metaphors and metonymy, oral, aural and visual, should be a universal part of any real education for the twenty-first century.

ALAN MACFARLANE

* * *

Finally, there is another dimension which arises from the prolif-
eration and ease of instant communication. This concerns the
conventions and the rules, the etiquette and the ethics, and also
the restraint involved with modern communication.

An analogy could be made with learning to drive a car and
pass a driving test. Cars are obviously lethal devices, which can
injure or kill people if driven badly. So we learn some of the
basics with an instructor and then take a test to see if we are
capable of going on the road. The same is true of even more
powerful tools on the Internet.

As much or more harm can be done by ignorance or malice
on the Internet, leading to psychological injuries, social rifts
and even deaths, as can be done with a car or motorbike. Yet
we do not treat learning to surf the web in the way we would
even deal with learning to surf the sea, let alone driving a car,
plane or boat.

There is, as far as I know, apart from one or two guides of a
technical kind concerned with ensuring that one's computer is
safe, no proper 'Highway Code' for the Internet. Without being
prescriptive, such a code should be devised and learnt by young
and old. Such things as courtesy, reading through what one puts
up, copyright, ethical issues, the difference of the private and
the public, the dangers of surveillance, the avoidance of risks
(pornography, crime, viruses and Trojans), there are a host of
types of advice that could be standardised, even though they
are always changing in this restless landscape.

I have had to learn all this by practice, as has each user, and
I am constantly having to learn new practices, for example

how to deal with strangers, people from other cultures with other conventions, what to answer and what to avoid, how to recognise spam. Yet not a single part of this whole new area was ever discussed, even at the rarefied level of Cambridge University, in the years up to 2009 and my retirement. I doubt whether it is yet.

Even some classes where young people are encouraged to share their experiences and anxieties, given some guidance and models, tips and warnings, could save a vast amount of anguish, inefficiency and misunderstanding.

We now live in a crowded cyber world where virtual cars, trucks, bikes and pedestrians are trying to cohabit the digital space. It is far more complicated than driving on a crowded motorway and now absorbs more of human brainpower and time than real driving. We should be being instructed on how to prepare ourselves for this virtual highway through the clouds of digital data.

* * *

This takes me to the last point. When I was young there were 'bookworms' at school, that is children who seemed to spend all their leisure time engrossed in reading comics and books. The imagined and fantasy worlds of adventure seemed far more appealing than the grim, dull, realities of school or many people's homes and lives. These bookworms sometimes verged on information junkies or addicts – restless and anxious when away from their comics and adventure books.

If this was a temptation and addiction with written materials, it is not difficult to understand what is now widely recognised as one of the strong features of our time – addiction to the virtual world of television, computers, smart phones, 'Second Worlds' and gaming. I feel it myself, pining to check my emails after a few hours absence from them, excited at the prospect of new messages. Yet I have this addiction in a mild form, not having anything but an ancient Nokia mobile, no iPad, many spaces in my house and outhouses with no connected devices.

Yet as I look at my young friends and family, they are almost constantly checking their devices – receiving or sending messages, chuckling and exclaiming, living in parallel and imaginative worlds with circles of friends, or addictively checking the latest sports, political, cultural or other events around the world.

This is something new in scale and kind, though foreshadowed by the book. It is likely to become ever more enticing and addictive when receiving and sending messages becomes even easier – with watch-like devices, screens in the corner of our glasses, or by simple cameras attached to, or even implanted in, us. We may well, some are already predicting, be able to walk around and see and speak to anyone from anywhere with no need for the Internet, computers, or smartphones.

The fragmentation of attention, the invasion of privacy, the constant disturbance of longer-term concentration, the rudeness to those we are with, who realise that our minds and our eyes are elsewhere, all these are effects of this new world. They change the way in which people think and interact.

As the load of emails and other types of messages, on Facebook, Twitter or other platforms, surges upwards, to make politics and speech something far more complicated, we are dimly aware of what is happening. But as far as I know, there is no equivalent to even basic advice about other forms of addiction or diseases which we have given early in our lives.

We may be taught at some schools about smoking, drinking, unsafe sex, drugs, pornography. We may learn about how to avoid certain basic diseases, food allergies and dietary disasters. But where is the instruction about the problems posed by new machines which appeal to the most human and powerful of drives – curiosity and the imagination?

Again, just some serious discussions about the issues, along with some suggested guidelines, might save minds and even lives. There are already equivalents to Alcoholics Anonymous in China and elsewhere, trying to detoxify Internet junkies. Why not prevent them reaching that stage by serious preparation for our age? This would obviously involve parents as well as children in courses on surviving the world of the cloud.

SIX

Cultures and Multi-Culturalism

T HROUGHOUT HISTORY, THERE has been huge mixture and overlap of peoples – traders, merchants, travellers, migrants, refugees. A multi-cultural world is nothing new. Yet it is also the case that for several reasons we now live in a world where we are having swiftly to come to terms with a situation of mixing and potential confrontations which feels new in scale, if not unprecedented.

When I was growing up in Britain in the 1950's, I would seldom encounter people of different civilisations and cultures. The restaurants and shops seemed mainly to be English, the faces were familiar white faces. Since then, and particularly in the last twenty years, England has changed. And the same is obviously true of many parts of the world.

Globalisation, meaning that numerous people move temporarily or permanently for economic (labour migration), educational or other reasons is clearly one reason for this. Mass tourism and growing wealth is another. There is also, as we know, a huge refugee crisis which is affecting Europe in particular, but also elsewhere, again not unprecedented in the World Wars or after the Vietnam War, but possibly in the future on a scale hitherto unknown.

As well as the fact that many people are suddenly finding

their towns and villages increasingly filled with people from around the world with different customs and cultures, there is a flood of virtual cultural contacts. The immense growth in trade, television, the internet, all present people daily with new minor shocks of unfamiliar places, their styles and assumptions.

How can we think about some of the practical ways in which we can deal with this threat to older identities and the inevitable clashes between the expectations of different cultures? These identity challenges are just part of a shifting world of gender, race, class and religious changes which leave people confused and sometimes hostile. Living in a multi-cultural world is one of the largest challenges of our times and a few reflections on how to face this are worth noting.

* * *

One way to think of it is through the idea that none of us have a single identity, but rather we have multiple identities, nested on top of each other in a kind of pyramid structure, becoming larger and larger in their scope but not conflicting. A resident in a part of London may, depending on the context, define him or her self as belonging to a certain street, a certain borough, a Londoner, English, British, European, Western. Or again they may say they are Jewish, middle-class, a doctor, a football player. We all have multiple roles and statuses.

The idea of lower-level identities, which merge at the next level up, is the basis of much of our life, and it is how all complex organisations tend to work. You are divided by difference at one level, but united at the level above, as in an army or business company.

This is and was the basis for the largest bureaucratic organisation in world history – the Chinese Empire - which through the Confucian education system and Confucian bureaucracy built up from the individual, to the family, to the village, to the county, to the province, to the Empire. A person can be a member of all these levels in different capacities. So this is one of the mechanisms for multiculturalism, and it is epitomised by China.

This partly solves one major problem with multiculturalism, for you can be a Nigerian, a West African, an African, a Muslim and an American all at the same time. There is no necessary contradiction. You can support India against England in the cricket tests, yet still fight for Queen and Country and feel British.

* * *

Here is a start, yet it is not as simple as this, and there are many ambiguities and contradictions which complicate the idea of 'levels' of identity. It may be that lower-level identities and loyalties are much stronger, and people refuse to forego them in relation to a higher level when there is a conflict between levels. This loyalty to lower levels is in fact normal. In almost all societies your loyalty to your family, clan and co-villagers outweighs abstract loyalties to a province, county, state or empire.

England was exceptional in basing its law on the assumption that people would come into a court and give true evidence which might incriminate their friends, neighbours or even family. The more normal situation is shown by China, for at the heart of Confucianism there is the idea that if it comes to a conflict between your loyalty to your lowest level relationship, your father, and your highest level, the Emperor you should betray the Emperor and pay filial duty to your father.

If the state asks you to 'inform' on members of your family who are suspected to be criminals, or even potential terrorists, what are you to do? Does abstract citizenship come before the bonds of blood and friendship?

This leads into a further clash, for while I have ended the hierarchy at the highest point on earth – the King, Emperor, President – much of the tension that continues to exist lies in the fact that, certainly in the monotheistic religions, or the international ideologies such as communism, your highest allegiance is to something beyond the state. If God is at the top, what happens when there is a clash of duties between God and the ruler?

This was particularly apparent to those who were invaded by Western religions, for example to the Japanese and Chinese when the missionaries arrived. These missionaries bought a monotheistic God who demanded a person's ultimate loyalty.

The Protestant movements in Christianity were centrally concerned with trying to make a split between private belief and conscience and public acceptance of the secular power. Yet even there, from very early on, there were clashes – famously in the 17th century when Quakers, Baptists and others were imprisoned for not showing sufficient loyalty to the Crown.

So the idea of 'levels' gives us a tool to think with and to accept that the restriction of a person to one level of allegiance to the exclusion of others is a ridiculous oversimplification. Yet it does not eliminate the problem of the conflict of loyalties altogether, especially in relation to fundamentalist, monotheistic, religions, or international political ideologies.

ALAN MACFARLANE

* * *

Another way to think about diversity combined with integration is by another analogy, this time in relation to games. Here we can think of the separation between the rules which bind us – political, economic and social – which have to be agreed upon and uniform – and the rules concerning expression and communication – culture, style, language, beliefs, which are highly variable and a matter of individual choice. This is the distinction between the rules ('whom you can marry', the social, economic and political laws we must share) and the playing of the game ('what you wear at your wedding', the culture and customs by which you live, including material culture and religion).

Such a distinction was essential in huge and diverse Empires and now, when somewhere like Britain or the United States is an internal empire of diversity, it is essential too. Its nature comes out when we compare it to its opposite – Japan and parts of continental Europe – where culture and society have traditionally been merged and hence uniformity of social and culture are essential.

The continental European solution is one where culture (what you believe, wear, eat, drink, speak) and society (politics, economics, social relations) are merged. As in the French case, it is possible to turn anyone into a French man or woman but only if they adopt the whole French cultural-social package and become French. Religion, education, language, styles all are part of what is needed to be fully accepted.

In the Anglosphere, at least in theory, the highly atomistic, contractual and individualistic system allows for similarity and difference. The rules of the game, politics, society, law, economics, are enforced uniformly across the civilisation. People must pay their taxes, obey the laws and accept the political system. Some basic tenets are not negotiable – individual rights, equalities, freedoms. But beyond that, as long as people play by the rules, their culture is their own affair.

* * *

Yet there are serious ambiguities here also. It is obvious that there are constant borderline cases. There are many examples, particularly in the treatment of women. For example, if it is your custom to practice foot binding and breaking of girl's feet, or the immolation of widows (suttee), or keeping women locked away (harem) or female genital mutilation, is this a matter which is cultural or social and should it be allowed? In these extreme cases, it may not be too difficult to drop cultural relativism and to appeal to universal standards. But it is not difficult to find much greyer areas.

For example, what about arranged marriage, or polygamy, or (to some people provocative) religious parades, or certain forms of eating and killing of animals, or clothing in public places? As we face the increasing mix of cultures and traditions, such borderline cases become ever more common and the wonder is how well, on the whole, people have adapted to them – even, in Britain, to the allowing of Sikhs to carry ritual daggers or wear turbans instead of crash helmets on motorbikes. Yet it is good to be reminded that the distinction between social rules and cultural styles is not watertight.

* * *

A third strategy which has softened the edges of the contact of peoples lies in the area of memory and the re-writing of the past. For many thousands of years civilisations and smaller groups have not been separated from each other. There has been a huge movement of people, ideas and things along roads, seas, through the mountains and forests, and nowadays over electronic communications. 'Purity' of race or nation is a fiction, imagined, invented, to make us close or distant from others. There is no such thing as a 'pure' American. Nor can you have a 'pure' Japanese, or a 'pure' Han Chinese (my Chinese 'Han' friends all have Manchu, Mongol or ethnic minority ancestors). As for the British, we are one of the most hybrid of all. In my own case, I have only recently discovered that I am not the Englishman (Anglo-Saxon) or Scotsman I thought I was for most of my life, but, on investigating my ancestors in detail, I find I am also Welsh, Scandinavian, German, Dutch, Spanish and perhaps with a touch of Indian, Burmese and Jamaican.

This hybridity is not just one of race, but also of all our cultural characteristics and is one of the reasons why the Scotsman David Hume commented that there was no such thing as a national character mixture in England. Americans, like all other civilisations, including English or Scots, are a 'fiction', as Daniel Defoe put it – we are all mongrels and mixes, bricolages and bundles. Our imagined communities are invented and constructed to make life tolerable and bear little relation to real 'facts'. It is important to realise this before we essentialise our differences, which leads to a ghetto mentality, a need to wall and fence and repel the threatening 'Other' who is, in fact, probably a distant cousin of some kind.

So how do we do this – cover over the trails which lead us

to ourselves, learning the 'Art of Forgetting'. Basically it is about suppressing some memories, re-inventing forgotten traditions, inventing commonalities. Many analysts have shown that our idea of 'America' or 'Britain' or 'France' is a recent invention. Diverse roots, ancient differences and uncomfortable past events are forgotten, and a mythical genealogy is built up uniting people. This helps absorption, for though large numbers of immigrants may maintain their cultural plurality, they may also very quickly readjust their past to fit their present. So they become British or American, as incoming groups have done over the centuries.

* * *

When people from different civilisations, or even from other cultures within a civilisation (Hungarians and Spanish, or even Scottish and English) interact, there are numerous potential clashes on the border of what liberty each individual has to pursue their own cultural norms. The question of the limits of liberty were partially addressed by John Stuart Mill's famous suggestion that we are free to do anything we like, as long as it does not infringe another's freedom. If we examine this, however, we realise that it does not get us very far. It gives Robinson Crusoe on his island absolute freedom before Man Friday turns up, but almost everything the rest of us do (or don't do) in some way or other impacts on others.

The endless quarrels, between neighbours, within the family, in business, provide numerous examples. Drinking, smoking, what we wear, how we speak, quickly take us into contested areas where I may want to smoke, get drunk, be naked, or utter racist or traitorous words, but this impacts on others.

How can this conflict be resolved beyond a mechanistic cost-benefit, utilitarian, calculus? If I benefit greatly by having my constantly barking dogs, and my neighbours are only inconvenienced when they go outside into their garden, my freedom can be thought to outweigh theirs. Yet it is not always a matter of cost-benefit balancing harms and all rules having fuzzy edges.

Particularly difficult in relation to Mill's formulation is control of the self. Suicide, over-eating leading to serious obesity, drug abuse, serious sado-masochism, watching child-pornography and other private behaviour is not purely personal but affects others. When we add in the harm we do to the general environment, pollution and degradation, and to animals and plants, it becomes an almost impossible tangle of contested liberties.

* * *

A related minefield concerns tolerance and intolerance. We start with the premise of tolerating others, their actions and their words. I disagree or even hate what you say, but I will defend to the death your right to say it. Yet there soon comes a point that tolerating what we consider intolerance becomes impossible. Our own tolerance has to turn to intolerance to preserve itself. An extreme form is if someone threatens to kill you. If you tolerate and do not resist, as a pacifist, your own tolerance is extinguished and intolerance triumphs in your death.

So there must be situations where you become intolerant in order to preserve wider tolerance – intolerant of rape, murder, drug dealing, in order to preserve 'our' freedoms. Again the lines and interpretation shift in the sand when applied at the international level. Can we tolerate North Korea having a nuclear bomb, or the Islamic state wanting to establish sharia law and the caliphate? Can we tolerate the international arms or drug or people trafficking trades?

* * *

As with war, it is not conceivable that we will be able to eradicate tensions and misunderstandings. Even between people who love each other and have come to understand the other over many years, there are moments of anger and misunderstanding. How much more so between the huge confusion of fast amalgamating civilisations.

Yet we can mitigate some of the effects through understanding each other a little better and even learning to love each other a little, or at least to admire and be amused by each other. At least that is my hope. Fear and ignorance, at least, can be decreased, and a world in which we are going to have to live for centuries to come in a set of relations which are unprecedented may be made a little more harmonious.

This requires active policies to promote mutual understanding and integration. This is already happening in many nurseries and kindergartens and schools around the world where people of different backgrounds learn to grow with each other. It is important to break other exclusivity in churches, mosques, clubs and other meeting places. Sport, television, popular culture, tourism, clothes, food and other mass consumption patterns are already doing this to a huge extent. The goal is not to blend people into one boring uniform mass, but to celebrate but also tolerate and understand difference.

SEVEN

Education and Life

I F WE BRIEFLY look at the role of 'education', in the wider sense, as a training for life, we can see that the systems used to inform and conform young people have changed and varied hugely. They reflect all aspects of a civilisation and its view of the past, present and future. Education reflects and shapes the religious, ethical, social, economic and political nature of the society or civilisation. Hence its huge importance both as an index of much else, and, as a society changes, as a shaper or adaptor to new worlds.

This role is derived from the varied functions of education. Education is used as a way to pass on knowledge and skills from previous generations. It is used to teach discipline and interpersonal relations. It is used in many societies as a way of keeping children occupied and safely guarded while their parents are away from home at work. It is sometimes used to teach people thinking skills which will make them flexible and creative when facing new challenges.

Through most of history, education was by word-of-mouth and dependent on memory. Books were expensive and scarce so that in essence the teacher held all the relevant knowledge in his or her head and passed it on, through rote learning, into the brains of the children. There was also craft education, where the master would demonstrate and comment on the making of objects by his pupil or apprentice.

Thus most schooling in the great traditions of Confucianism, Buddhism and Islamic learning has largely consisted of sitting pupils in rows and, sometimes with the aid of simple textbooks derived from ancient sages or prophets, passing on to them the great truths of the past so that they can, in turn, pass these on and at least have a grasp of the simple tools of reading, writing and counting.

The aim is not to teach the art of thinking in the sense of logic, analytics, rhetoric, mathematics. It is not the tools which explain how to receive information and then make decisions as to how to use it that are being taught. That is, the teaching is not in the art of argument, of selection, of discrimination between truth and falsehood, the art of intuition, proof, arranging knowledge over time in order to solve large problems or to guess at new things or create inventions.

All such skills are unnecessary since there is nothing new to be discovered – the great truths having been elaborated by Confucius, the Buddha, Mohammed or to a certain extent, Aristotle. Students are also to be discouraged from a form of thinking which would give them freedom, challenging what they learnt, thinking new thoughts subversive of closed systems and contesting the authority of elders, parents and the religious and political establishment. Education is learning the disciplines necessary to take one's place in a fixed world.

This roughly describes the majority of systems of education. Elements of such a system can still be found over much of the world. There are also hidden pressures to move towards such a closed educational system in any civilisation. As we shall see, there is such a tendency in advanced capitalist societies to revert to this education for submission and conformity.

* * *

There is, however, an alternative education which many people trace back to the Greeks with their emphasis on the Socratic method of question-and-answer, debates, the learning of logic and rhetoric, geometry and philosophy. This unusual approach was transmitted through Roman and early Islamic writings to medieval Europe. Here there grew up the schools and univer-sities in what we recognise as a more disputatious, contested, open, educational system.

My own learning was for an unpredictable professional future where I might end up as anything – a lawyer, artist, teacher, soldier, politician, businessman, civil servant, explorer. So I needed generic skills – not the subset needed to be a Confucian Mandarin, a Buddhist monk, an Islamic mullah or merchant, or a French civil servant. I needed to be taught all that was required of the social, mental, moral and bodily skills and practices which might help me to succeed in an open and highly mobile world.

I was to be trained for many things: to learn how to enjoy my leisure through the appreciation of art, music, poetry, games and hobbies. How to learn to communicate effectively through writing, speaking and if necessary acting, dancing and sports, so that I would impress and persuade others. I was to learn to be ethically upright so that I not only felt at ease with myself, but earned the trust of others. I was to learn to become respon-sible and mature, so that I could become a stable adult, parent and grandparent. I was to learn to get on well with people of all backgrounds, to bring out the best in them. I was to work effectively as a team player as well as an individual.

In other words I was to become the epitome of a combination of a Greek philosopher, Spartan athlete, French savant, English gentleman, Confucian Mandarin and medieval Christian monk. This kind of education was in the past expensive and privileged, though elements of it were found well beyond the British private schools and Oxbridge. As an ideal, it was spread across the British Empire, also to the United States, though one of its strongest methods, the shutting away of children in boarding schools, was less widely copied.

* * *

My own education, the combination of many strands of the peculiar English system based on sending children away from home literally, or virtually, in their early teens to become members of the wider society, is part of a wider pattern. The background is of a particular class system, Protestant religion, imperial legacy, civil society, market capitalist economy and democratic polity. And of course in my case took place over half a century ago in a different world. It needs to be rethought in the context of the next fifty years of the 21st-century, a present world already so different from my own youth.

Some of the current and future challenges have been outlined in previous chapters. It has become clear that children, and increasingly throughout their lives to keep up to date in a changing world and to enable them to take control of their lives, people will need to be trained for a world where the main part of one's life will not be concerned with traditional work, but with 'leisure' or at least service and creative activities.

It will be a world where thinking machines and new computer-based communication systems will dominate our lives. We will have vast new potentials with the Internet, but also huge new distractions and threats from the temptations and exhilaration of the virtual world. All of this is highly relevant to how we educate.

We will be living in a world where the threats of war, and particularly the new kinds of subversive war linked to terrorism, lead to restrictions of our liberties, a growth in surveillance and power of the state. We will be living in a world where the old models of government, the extreme positions of British Parliamentary or American democracy on the one hand, and the single party state on the other, are interfused. Hopefully new forms of participatory, civil society based, localised, life will flourish.

We will be living in a world where the three billion people who inhabited the planet when I went to university, has risen to between nine and twelve billion by the second half of this century. The cities will be huge with the movement from the countryside, the countryside will also be densely populated. The pressing population may have solved some of the problems of ecological damage and global warming, though perhaps not all, thus again causing strife and tension.

We will be living in a crowded world with ever increasing mixture of cultures and backgrounds. This will not just be the physical mixing of peoples in the streets and markets, but the hybrid, contested, virtual worlds of the digital age.

It will be a world where people live on average thirty years longer than was common in my youth – bringing new problems of what to do after any specific career or job, and how to deal with new pressures on the health services.

Much else will be changing. The sharp identities we assume, of a national, sexual, racial, kind are swiftly shifting. Relations between the old and the young, men and women, people of different backgrounds are in turmoil.

* * *

Given all this, how should we think about a sensible education system for the next half-century?

We should first note that the slide towards a system similar to that introduced as a solution for the health crisis, in other words the application of American business models, or even the supposed factory production methods of the top Shanghai mathematics academies, is not the way to go.

It does not work to produce a rounded and properly educated child, but rather creates human robots, taught by anxious and overstretched teachers, conformist and unimaginative. This is the last thing our rapidly changing world needs. We can make machine robots, and our children should be something else.

Nor, as I noted with health, is it even efficient in its own terms, for the obsession with bureaucracy, administration, league tables, standardised tests and results means that teachers have even less time to teach, and general ignorance grows. As we look at the mostly disastrous reforms introduced into the British state education system over the last ten years, we understand why it is that sensible Chinese are not sending their children, on the whole, to the state schools, but to the best private schools. These

schools have managed, through high fees, and some independence, to preserve some of the real education, the training of
the mind, body, heart and spirit, which I experienced.

Yet even the best schools need to adapt and certainly we need
to think of how to organise a much wider range of schools, not
just in the West, but in the swiftly developing educational worlds
of China, India and elsewhere.

* * *

I vividly remember a friend, an engineer and scientist, stress-
ing the huge leap from the early nineteenth century world of
individual geniuses and inventors, who could master the whole
of the knowledge base and skills needed to make significant
progress in their subject (chemistry, engineering or whatever),
to the contemporary situation where so many interlocking skills
are needed that only team-work can succeed in making complex advances.

Of course team-work has always been present in many professions and occupations, the army, navy, factories, universities.
But it is now true of most intellectually based progress.
I have increasingly found this to be true in my own projects. All
require small groups working well together to achieve results
which no single person would be able to deliver. The skills are
just too complex.

So there is a huge need for young people to be taught how to
work effectively with others in collaborative teams. Hence the
value of team games and sports, musical and artistic groups,
adventure groups, problem-solving groups, group discussion and
brain-storming, debates and drama. These skills, which were

very much stressed in my own schooling, should be developed in primary schools of the future.

* * *

The education of a young Chinese or other citizen of most countries in the nineteenth and twentieth centuries was based on local skills, connections and knowledge. Britain was a bit different because of its Empire, but even there was an emphasis on local citizenship.

The world is now global and international. Most successful people work between cultures. They need to be rooted in one tradition, but also to be prepared to travel, both physically and in the mind, to other worlds. This should be taught through education.

Three possible ways of achieving this are:

a.   *Teaching an equivalent of anthropology at schools. Anthropology is centred on the skills of inter-cultural understanding through systematic analysis and immersion in other cultures. It is about cultural translation. It teaches respect for the other and provides some tools for helping us to overcome cultural differences.*

b.   *Systematic encounters with other cultures through supervised overseas expeditions, or by visiting different sub-cultures within one's own civilisation – anything which creates a cultural shock and forces one to re-evaluate one's own assumptions.*

c.   *Pairing with single students or classes or schools in other cultures, both at the individual level (Facebook-type friends), and through institutional pairing, for example each class paired with a school class in Africa, India, Burma, America, U.K.*

d. *A systematic course of reading, films, music etc. from cultures outside one's own.*

e. *Language learning*

* * *

The main intellectual communication technology up to 1950 was the written word (or mathematical symbol). Almost all instruction at school was based around learning to read and write. All that has changed. We gain over three quarters of our information about the world now through visual images, whether TV, the Internet, Films or whatever.

As yet, as pointed out earlier, little instruction is given to children about how to 'read' visual media, or how to 'write' films (the best way of learning how to understand them). This should be corrected. So there should be courses in:

a. *Interpreting visual images, whether films or television or the internet (Youtube etc)*

b. *How to write films, not only how to film and edit and put up film on the Internet, but how to set up websites etc. All the skills of a visual anthropologist should be developed - an interest in filming, photography, art, painting, design and other communication skills of a visual kind, including a basic history of art and media, should be encouraged.*

* * *

Most educational systems have traditionally been ways of reinforcing authority and of transmitting acceptable knowledge through the generations. Passing on 'wisdom', or at least some practical skills, has been the purpose. This top-down model is now no longer appropriate. Most people can learn what they need to know in the way of facts from the Internet.

So what is needed now is the teaching of skills in searching out, assessing and using information, not just in books and articles as I learnt, but mainly through online databases. Search systems, collating of information, doing projects of a multimedia kind, this is what young people should be taught about.

All this requires something like the child-centred problem-solving approach which we saw at an experimental school in Shandong Province in China, where the teachers were enablers, guides, mentors, rather than knowledge repositories. The method used by a good undergraduate teacher in the final year at University, or a Ph.D. supervisor – like a pilot on a ship – is the model.

* * *

Basically overlapping, but conceptually a little distinct, the new world is one where technology is moving so fast and having such an enormous effect, that we become slaves to it if we do not understand and hence control it.

So our children should be being instructed on how technology works and how to deal with it in our lives. For example, there should be courses in social media, emailing, Skype, mobile phone use, computing in all aspects and other technologies. We should be teaching them the philosophy of computing and the internet and the ways in which technology more generally develops and works and controls our lives.

The work of Lewis Mumford, Marshall McLuhan and others should be taught and the effects of rapid technological change. My essay in Letters to Lily on 'How did we reach our digital age' has thoughts on all this, and especially on our need to preserve moments of silence, integrity, peace and concentration and not to be swept away and have our lives fragmented by too much exposure to technology.

Learning to read, to walk for pleasure, to have hobbies and interests away from machines, are all parts of this. The habits of self-discipline and control of our obsession and addiction with technology.

* * *

Finally, one of the hugest recent changes has been from a world based on the premise of inequality, whether gender, age, race, caste or class, to one of high social mobility and no birth-given inequalities. This is central to education.

Young people need to learn how to both respect and empathise with others, and to accord difference were it is due, and also to accept that others may know more than they do. But also not to slavishly follow leaders or be over-awed by power.

They need to learn to question and challenge, but also do this in a constructive and sympathetic way. In particular the handling of sexual, age and class differences, and differences in the family, need to be discussed and worked out.

All this has to be done in an increasingly relativistic world, where there are not necessarily any underpinning deities or absolutes. How to handle very rapid paradigmatic changes and bombardment of ideas in a postmodern world.

The model of education which I was brought up with was one whereby education was seen as something you went through early in life. It was a training or preparation for the real business of earning a living and adulthood. It was also a transition ritual from childhood, through adolescence, to maturity, in other words a 'rite of passage'.

All this is still the case, but the implications of what I have written suggest that we need to rethink the whole idea of education being an early-in-life package, once 'got through', no longer of real concern. There are several reasons for this. I shall mention three.

The first and obvious one is that our world is now changing so fast, as a result of technological, economic, social and ideological laws of exponential growth, that we need constant refreshing in our education. I have had the good fortune to have had such refreshing more or less automatically as a teacher in a top University where, year after year, new ideas have rushed into my consciousness through my students and colleagues. Each year a fresh intake injects new challenges and needs, and I have to 'keep up' with changing ideas in a changing world, especially across the continents through the teaching of anthropology.

Yet this will in the future be true of us all, whatever our activities. If we want to stay active and participate in our rapidly changing world we will need to 're-tool', 're-fresh', 're-expand' our minds. What we learnt thirty years ago will no longer be a sufficient set of tools for our current world. This is a big change even from my own childhood, where things moved slowly enough for one period of education to be enough for a long life.

A second new development is in the leisure society I described. In a world where most people will probably have little 'work', one of their main pleasures and sources of self-satisfaction could be through learning new things, and perhaps contributing themselves. While our bodies and our abilities to make things and to make money may not be necessary, our minds and emotions are infinitely expandable. Already we know this from our experience of taking up new hobbies, travelling to new place, watching new films and reading new books. Expanding lifelong education could build on this and open up ever more new and exciting areas for exploration.

In the spirit of moving activities back to the lower, local, levels, and with the greater personal leisure, it would also be worth exploring much more 'home' learning. That is to say those who had skills and interests to pass on to young people – parents, grandparents, friends, neighbours – could set up collaborative and co-operative teaching units (duly vetted of course) to help to teach each other's children. This has often happened informally in history. Now is a new opportunity to think about this again.

Thirdly, there is the change in longevity. Some years ago Peter Laslett became interested in what he called 'The Third Age' and saw the potentials of education for making it a much more interesting period by helping to set up the highly influential 'University of the Third Age', movement in Britain. Retired people with a particular skill or passion offer to give classes in their special interest – painting, walking, local history, quantum theory, languages or literature. Whatever it was, people could sign up to their courses, workshops or tours.

This idea can be extended further at all levels and not confined to academic subjects, but include all crafts (pottery, gardening), sports and games. The sharing, sociality and friendship is part of it, but it is also deeply educational. So as much true 'education' could go on in the Third (and Fourth) ages, as in the first and second.

The practical way to make this possible is to think of free education as an entitlement, part of the package which would form the baseline in a reasonably affluent society. Just as a basic living wage could be paid to all, so there would coupons or entitlements to the other things which we need – house, health and education. These coupons would ensure a basic amount of all of these – and only if wanted more than this basic entitlement, and made a successful case for this need, or were prepared to make some sacrifice of time and energy, would you get more.

* * *

All of these are part of schooling. For in encouraging a wide education with new elements we should avoid the danger of throwing out much that was good in the old - language learning, basic numeracy and literary skills, encountering new and exciting disciplines and ideas. Nor should we ever forget that almost all of our education comes through people, most of them not our school teachers, but friends and family.

EIGHT

War and Peace

T HE DAILY HORRORS of war as we see them on our
screens and hear of them in other media, are enough to
remind us of the pain, destruction and waste of war. War was
thought to be the worst of all tragedies by Thomas Malthus,
for it brought with it famine and disease, as it still does today.

Millions have died and suffered appalling wounds, civilisations have been destroyed, it all seems pretty pointless, yet it
continues. If we have another World War we will probably
destroy the planet. So it is a subject we cannot avoid. Yet it is
a huge and complex topic. How can we proceed briefly here
and make some sort of contribution?

What I will do is to survey briefly the history of previous and
current attempts to bring about the end of war and to suggest
some of the reasons for their failure. I will then make some blue
skies suggestions as to how we could re-think our strategies in a
world which is more inter-connected than ever before, yet more
awash with weapons, many of them capable of destroying the
world. It is tempting to leave the subject on one side, yet to fail
to think about it, is to collude in the present and future tragedies.

* * *

As we watch the collapse of much of the belt from North Africa to Afghanistan into chaos, which apparently no one can do much about, as well as dangerous confrontations on the borders of Russia and China, we feel that we are at another time of the dissolution of the old rules – and hence require new ones.

If we look at the political relations between distinct and independent nation-states and civilisations we can single out certain turning points when serious attempts have been made to devise a framework to avoid conflict, to invent new rules for the political game. These frameworks have worked intermittently and partially but then broken down.

Leaving out much of history, let us start with one famous attempt to create a set of rules for international relations, the Peace of Westphalia of 1648. In this a number of exhausted European nations, after a mass slaughter which had laid much of Europe to waste for thirty years, tried to devise a new framework for peace. The terms of this arrangement are simple and can be summarised in two rules. No state can attack another independent and sovereign state. And all states, whatever their size and power, are to be treated as equal.

Of course this did not stop interminable wars, culminating dramatically in the great Napoleonic Wars of the end of the eighteenth and early nineteenth centuries, but at least the treaty was there as a kind of beacon or standard. It lay behind appeals such as that of Immanuel Kant in 1795 in his 'To Perpetual Peace; A Philosophical Sketch'. His simple rules were:

1. No treaty of peace that tacitly reserves issues for a future war shall be held valid.

2. No independent nation, be it large or small, may be acquired by another nation by inheritance, exchange, purchase, or gift.

3. Standing armies shall be gradually abolished.

4. No national debt shall be contracted in connection with the foreign affairs of the nation.

5. No nation shall forcibly interfere with the constitution and government of another.

6. No nation at war with another shall permit such acts of war as shall make mutual trust impossible during some future time of peace.

Kant's suggestions were largely ignored. Yet the second half of the nineteenth century was, within Europe, apart from some terrible events such as the Crimean War and the Franco-Prussian War of 1870, relatively peaceful.

Yet these older rules, applying to a set of middle-sized European states were always vulnerable to the growing system of alliances of the newly industrialising, highly militarised and excessively nationalistic entities emerging over the Continent. The whole system more or less collapsed with the First World War in 1914.

It was immediately realised that a new set of rules, enforced by a body above the level of individual nation-states, was needed to try to avert another such war. In the first two weeks of the War, Goldsworthy Lowes Dickinson sketched out a plan for what he soon termed 'The League of Nations'. His ideas were expanded and modified by a committee on which he sat, and formed the basis for the future League.

Dickinson was a pacifist and his internationalism and interest in a high level organisation stemmed in part from his recent travels through America, India, China and Japan. This led him to believe in the common humanity and dignity of man and to feel particularly shocked by the carnage which was starting to occur. He believed that a club or league of all nations could be formed, where rules could be enforced to prevent further wars.

The League was officially launched in 1920, but from the start was fatally flawed in various ways. Firstly, the United States refused to join and this very substantially weakened it. Secondly the punitive attitude towards the losers in the war, which was castigated by Dickinson's fellow Kingsman and friend, John Maynard Keynes, in his devastating Economic Consequences of the Peace (1919), sowed the seeds for another war. Linked to this was the refusal to let Germany join the League at the start, which was bound to cause huge bitterness and, later, tragedy.

Thirdly, the League had no monopoly of force and no certain source of funding. As Mussolini boasted, 'the League is very well when sparrows shout, but no good at all when eagles fall out.' Contributions to the League were voluntary so it only had limited resources of money and arms. So it failed to avert the rearmament and the rise of the biggest eagle of all, Germany, and the consequent Second World War.

That war showed that some kind of world mechanism must again be devised to bind together nations and to avert another World War. So the United Nations was founded within months of the end of the War, using some of the ideas and assets of the League. There were some improvements on the League of Nations, in particular the United States was a central member and funder of the organisation and it had a much wider membership. It also had a firmer way of raising funds and a broader humanitarian remit.

So it was patchily successful, despite tragic failures which are well known. But ultimately it again depended on unanimity in the Security Council to take large-scale action, and the most powerful States were often unwilling to pass resolutions, especially during the Cold War.

Yet until the end of the twentieth century, the United Nations, combined with fragments of the Westphalian idea of independent sovereignty was sufficient for many of us to feel some hope. We were also comforted by the end of the Cold War and the predominance of an apparently benign United States. We felt we had reached some kind of plateau of safety.

Since the start of this millennium, partly triggered by the bombing of the Twin Towers on 9/11, and then given depth by the invasion of Iraq and Afghanistan and subsequent invasions into other Middle Eastern states, we have been shocked into a new instability.

Tony Blair in 1999 had set out a new, 'post-Westphalian' 'doctrine of the international community', arguing that globalization had made the Westphalian approach anachronistic. Along with President George Bush the younger he was formulating the new doctrine that humanitarian motives, and ideological beliefs concerned with universal human rights (which could well include the forced promotion of democracy) overrode national sovereignty.

This in turn, since the U.N. Security Council was split between Communist and Democratic nations, meant that the decision of one or more leading world powers overrode the vote of the United Nations. So Bush and Blair were prepared to break Westphalia and the United Nations with the Invasion of Iraq.

After that huge event, there has been no answer to any country which decides it is in their ideological, economic or political self-interest to attack another, especially if they can claim that they feel under some kind of threat of attack. We are back in the Thirty Years War, but on a global scale and with nuclear weapons.

In such a situation there are two principal ways in which we, in the West, can react – drawing in on ourselves, or pushing out to understand the rest of the world. The defensive approach basically consists of pulling up the drawbridge, strengthening our defences, trying to preserve what we perceive to be our own identity and wealth.

The other approach is to go out and try to do two things. One is to find out what, precisely, other civilisations are, try to understand them in their own terms to see what sort of threat 'they' might pose to 'us' and 'we' to 'them', and how much we have in common.

The second is, once we have established how the world works at a civilisational level, to try to set out a new, global, set of institutions and rules that avoids the inadequacies of Westphalia, the League and the United Nations. In other words to build institutions of a new kind, in conditions which have hitherto never existed before, that is to say a proper Harmony of Nations, harmony in the Confucian sense of accepting difference and living with it, not in the sense of uniformity.

* * *

Einstein's aphorism, 'Problems cannot be solved at the same level of thinking that created them', explains how centuries of bloody war in Europe were suddenly brought to a halt by the creation of the European Union. Francois Monnet, whose vision shaped the Union, realised that to solve the problem of endless clashes, it was necessary to widen the context. Monnet's genius was to widen the definition of 'Us'. He created a European context. We need to widen the horizons, to encourage people to think in a wider, comparative, and collaborative way.

The problems were created at the 'level of thinking' of the nation-state and before that of the state. Up to the Cold War, and that means the significantly titled United Nations, the unit of confrontation and analysis was the nation-state. The failure to find a way to control the nation-state is largely caused by the fact that the analysis remains at the level of the nation-state.

* * *

Most games and sports (and war can be seen as a violent game) require a referee or umpire who is outside the game and above the individual players. The rules of the game are accepted by the players and they implicitly delegate to the referee the power to enforce these rules by imposing penalties on players who infringe them. The League of Nations and the United Nations were set up to do this. Yet as long as America remained the sole superpower after the end of the Cold War, it could break the international rules (as in the invasion of Iraq without U.N. approval) and refuse to accept the rulings and jurisdiction of the International Court of Justice (along with India and China) accepted by almost all other countries.

The United States was like the big child in the playground, sufficiently powerful to boss or bully the smaller children. Such a child sees no virtue in a referee, except when such a referee, as with the IMF, WTO, or World Bank is heavily biased in its favour.

We now live in a multipolar world, and one where China will become the biggest child in the playground quite soon, so that the United States may well see that it is, after all, in its interest to have a referee. When there are six or seven roughly equal players, it is in all their interests to have the protection of an agreed mediator or referee.

The nature of such referees and the sanctions they have, basically the 'rule of law' which stipulates that everyone (even the most powerful) is to abide by the rules of the game and that all disputes are to be settled by due process of law, and not by physical force, is, of course not easy to agree on. Adam Smith's model of the 'night-watchman state', that is to say a non-intrusive person who patrols at night to see that all is working well, might be an idea for a world government. Such a night watchman is there, like all police and courts, not to interfere in the normal workings, but to intervene and protect when necessary.

Thus, in Smith's formulation, the night-watchman state should only deal with the very large universal problems – with things which stretch beyond the local level. Although Smith did not envisage this at the world civilisational level, it could scale up to deal with all the matters where we are bound together between civilisations, and where one of the actors' extreme behaviour is deeply affecting others. This might include the following.

- *Global warming and environmental degradation – including such 'commons' as the air, oceans, forests, mountains, deserts, rivers.*

- *International communications, including both physical communications such as ships, planes and railways and the electronic communications which are now so important.*
- *International illegal trading – including people smuggling, prostitution, drugs, arms dealing.*
- *International crime, including terrorism.*
- *International disputes – potential wars between nations and civilisations.*
- *Weapons control – particularly chemical, biological and nuclear.*

If each civilisation had representatives on the world body and that body, like the International Court, considered the conflicts and adjudicated or mediated, the due process of law and regulation might be achieved. There are of course dangers – bureaucratisation, delays, wounded pride, but either we do something like this, recognising our mutual involvement in a global world, or we are dead. We are back in a tribal world, but armed not with bows and arrows but nuclear, chemical and biological weapons.

* * *

The basic idea is a club, in other words one either applies to join or is asked to join by the members, after fulfilling certain conditions. In this way it is like the European Union (often described as a club). So it is voluntary and one can be expelled or leave it. Like a club is has a clubhouse and amenities. Like a club it has a name and a 'being'. Like a club it has rules and conventions about how one should make a contribution to it (financial or otherwise). Like a club it has elected officers. So far it is quite a bit like the United Nations but it would not be composed of nation-states but of civilisations.

Secondly it would be like a Trust. In other words trust and trusteeship would be involved – and a task – to save and improve the world in various ways would be its purpose as a trust.

Thirdly it would have elements of a game – it would be fun, it would administer world sports and cultural activities. The game would have rules and ways of playing that would bind people together.

Fourthly it would be like an orchestra, in that the different civilisations would be free to continue to play their own notes on their own instruments, but in harmony, as long as they maintained an agreed rhythm and scale.

Fifthly it would be ritualised – that is, it would have the binding power of rituals, words, sounds, costumes, panoply, repetition and symbolism which would both reduce difference and inequality (by being choreographed) and also affirm the relations between the disparate parts.

Sixthly, it would have elements of the division of labour of a body, in that the different civilisations would be principally responsible for different tasks – education, economy, culture, ecology and climate, poverty reduction.

* * *

The biggest question, of course, is how to recruit members. If it is too small it will not work, if it is too large likewise. The simplest membership would either be a fixed quota irrespective of size as in the UN, or proportional to size.

Another question is the control of force. It would not work unless it overcame the problem of the League and the United Nations which is that neither had the force sufficient to stand up to the eagles. It must be the biggest eagle.

Like the plan after the Second World War to ban all weapons (except those of the United States), it would ban all weapons except those held by the club. It must have a monopoly of force if it is to replace the state in the nation. It will take time – but this must be the goal.

* * *

There is bound to be opposition to this idea from various quarters. Among the predictable ones are:

a. *The United Nations will fear its position and role will be weakened. This may indeed be the case in the long run– where its goals will be better met. For a while the United Nations may well become more powerful.*

b. *The United States which opposes any organisation of the less powerful which might challenge its government – as recently with the 'World Development Fund' successfully launched by China and which the United States tried to squash. But there will be a time when the United States either has to join or be marginalised. So we need to push and dangle the membership prize.*

c. *Nation-states within civilisations where, like the nation-states within the European Union, may feel for a while that their sovereignty*

is diminished – as in the current European Union debate. That is fine. They will, as with the EU, finally see the benefits outweigh the costs.
***d**. Numerous marginal groups, most obviously fundamentalist groups such as ISIS who do not want an end to battle and fear. If the world comes together it will be frozen out of the present power structure.*
***e**. The arms industry, drug traffickers, international people smugglers and others who would be so restricted in their profiteering.*

So, one small step at a time. I just float the idea and then, if it has the right incentive structure, it will grow. This dream may not be attainable in the way I have specified, but if we fail to attempt to think of a new way for the world to move from our present, near-destructive situation, we are all dead, or, at the best, living in an Orwellian world of '1984', on 'a darkling plain where ignorant armies clash by night'.

What is certain is that current structures are not working or preventing wars. We need to think of all alternatives. The one above, raising the level of government one level, may not appeal to all, and others will call for the reverse – in line with the general downward delegation recommended in this book. This would return power to the nation-state, or whatever was the real body of collective sentiment. This would only cede minimal rights to a higher body – perhaps the control of nuclear and other powerful weapons and some kind of court to adjudicate disputes. Whether this would lead to a return to the pre-Westphalian 'war of all against all' is not clear. What we do know is that we need a new path.

Afterword

E ACH GENERATION FACES new challenges. The present and the foreseeable future are no worse than many past eras. Yet there are huge changes afoot, as I have argued, which will make for new kinds of difficulties. I have touched on those relating to computers, migration, changing health and longevity and others. To these can be added the loss of certainty and faith which seems to put our deepest assumptions in question.

What can I say to young people growing up in such an age, especially where the whole world seems to be changing very rapidly, especially fast in countries such as China, India and much of what used to be called the developing world which are trying to 'westernize' or 'modernize'?

Here are just a few things that have helped me in my search for a way of living. They buffer some of the stresses and strains and bring me internal peace and hope. They are in no particular order and the list could be extended and deepened, but this is a start.

There is friendship. Much can be dealt with by sharing with others, and most thoughts and activities are enriched by reflecting on them with friends. Our families may give us support and comfort, especially when we are young, but many find themselves rather alone as they grow into an adult world. Making a real effort to form, retain and build strong friendships I have found to be a real solace. The art is to find people we can trust, who have similar enthusiasms which we can share, who can see outside themselves, who treat us with affection and respect, which we reciprocate.

It is a craft or art which we learn from our infancy, and friendship can cause pain as well as happiness. Yet in what has been described as 'the lonely crowd', the increasingly individualistic and competitive world we live in can be made warmer and more meaningful if we have real, equal, and non-manipulative friendships.

A second thing I have learnt is humour. Life is often apparently bizarre, cruel, senseless, unfair. It can hit and hurt you. Yet I have found that humour – whether seeing the ridiculous, the hypocrisy and pretensions, the delightful irrationality, the unresolvable contradictions and paradoxes has helped. Laughter can bring down dictators and will make a private grief something that can be shared. Again humour is an art and craft and much of my education was teaching me to appreciate different forms of humour and the deeper lesson that life is far too serious to be taken entirely seriously.

Another lesson concerns the relations between mind, heart, spirit and body. They are all connected and each affects the other. In particular, I was brought up with the saying 'a sound mind in a sound body'. If your body is in bad condition, this is likely to drive down your mind (and vice versa). I certainly know that by doing the obvious minimal things, I have found happiness and contentment easier.

Watching what you eat and drink (moderation in all things – I do not eat red meat, do not drink much, do not smoke or take drugs) is essential. Many of the things we ingest shape our moods – for example drinking large quantities of tea (black, brown or green) is of enormous benefit in terms of energy, calmness and confidence.

Or again, enough exercise – at least twenty minutes reasonably fast walking each day, some body-loosening and calming exercises (ten minutes of simple yoga each day) not only adds to your lifespan, but is intellectually stimulating. Walking, as many have observed, is a huge aid to thought or, as Albert Einstein put it 'the legs of the wheels of invention'. Not getting too tired - sleeping properly, stopping to have rests every thirty minutes or hour at least in whatever one is doing, allowing enough and a little spare time for every job so that one is not stressed - makes life suddenly better.

Another thing I have found is the reflecting on my life, keeping a diary, noting down thoughts, filming life as it passes and watching the films, examining the life of my ancestors and parents, all helps me to put my own life into context. We tend to write fewer letters on paper nowadays, so need to make a special effort to replace this by personal self-observation and analysis. Treasuring the passing days by keeping a record of them, which will be a solace in older age, is also worthwhile.

I have always found it helpful to learn from others. The idea of a role model is especially important nowadays as the world changes so fast and increasing numbers of people in many rural areas outside the west are moving away from their fami¬lies. In relatively stable societies it might have been enough to watch parents and close relatives to see how to live. Now your parents often belong to a generation brought up in a different world and you may not be able to respect or even like them, and certainly they seem to have little sound guidance for you.

Yet there are many great figures in history who experience still has lessons for us today. I read, and write, biographies of such people, do film interviews with them, learn about how they faced difficulty and found fulfillment and how they improved their creativity. It is a interaction with people I have met and admired, from my first teachers up to my students today. These can be greatly supplemented by the vast wealth of extraordinary lives people have led in many different cultures.

One of the things which is happening is that different cultures are entering our living space and upsetting our beliefs and deepest and hitherto unquestioned assumptions. This is a challenge, but also an opportunity, for I have found that by becoming interested in how people in other civilisations and societies organise their lives, I find it easier to understand my own. I have found that educated travel – not only to other real places all over the world, or even the huge diversity most people can find on their doorsteps – but virtually, through the vast array of films and books about the world, is enormously stimulating and helpful.

I have also found an antidote to confusion and doubt is to look at history. We are often shocked into thinking that we live in the worst of times, that things are bleak and dark, that the world is currently in an unparalleled mess. A study of history (or even our past diaries) shows that although things do not repeat themselves exactly, they rhyme, as Mark Twain put it. There are patterns and tendencies and we can sort out our own experiences within a much longer context which helps us to understand and adapt. For while many may not believe in an ultimate God or heaven, we do not therefore have to believe that everything is meaningless chaos. Life is pretty orderly, in fact, and filled out with small satisfactions and repetitions.

The tricks and methods we develop are, of course, highly personal, and I am not sure how much of what I am writing will help you from your different worlds. All that I can say is that through friendship, love, the kindness of strangers, combined with trying to develop my self-confidence and trying to be kind and generous to others I have enjoyed my life. Leading a modest life which does as little damage to others in the world as possible, I have been enormously fortunate to reach an age (seventy-four) and a degree of peace, as I sit in a beautiful English garden on this June day, looking at the birds and roses.

Despite the deep tragedies around us, we should aim, in our modest ways, to make it possible for as many humans and other animals to live with such contentment. They should wake each morning with a sense of excitement, and end each day with a feeling of added richness. The only things which can stop this in our personal psychology are cynicism, hopelessness, lack of confidence. I was never very talented at anything as a child, but I learnt that almost anybody can do almost anything if they really know what it is they want to do and stick at it.

Good luck, and as they used to say in my culture, 'God speed'. To paraphrase - 'Humankind is born free. All we have to do is to recognise and throw off our chains.'

ALAN MACFARLANE

How We
Understand the World

THIS BOOK IS part of a series of short letters written to young friends. Encouraged by the reception of my *Letters to Lily* (2005), I decided to write a set of letters to her younger sister—Reflections for Rosa. I was then asked by other friends to write short books for their children.

In each I try to explore some aspect of 'How We Understand the World,' based on my experience as an anthropologist and historian at Cambridge University. I have tried to put into simple words what I have learnt about discovery, creativity and methods to understand our complex world.

EXPLORE THE SERIES

CAM RIVERS
PUBLISHING

Image on front cover is an adaptation of Caritas (Charity) by Pieter Bruegel the Elder, available in the public domain.